Diana Farr Louis

travels in
northern
GREECE

ATHENS NEWS

ISBN 960-86395-9-X

© Diana Farr Louis,
Athinaika Nea S.A., 2006
All rights reserved

Published by Athens News
3, Christou Lada Str.
Athens 102 37
www.athensnews.gr

Publisher's Preface

The chapters of this book were originally published as travel features in the *Athens News*, Greece's historic, English-language newspaper. They are presented here updated and re-worked, and with some new photography.

Diana Farr Louis has lived in Greece and written about it for over thirty years. Thanks to this long-term view, time and place in her writing elide, as indeed they do in life. An ancient temple, a wooded glen, a stormy beach are never separate from our experience of them. It is a moment that pins a place to our memory like a collected rare moth.

In an age of package holidays, all-inclusives and enclosed resorts – when tourists dictate their terms, be it a swimming pool, golf course or menu item – the point of travelling elsewhere is obfuscated. And thanks to travel books packed with practical information, telegraphic descriptions and price quotations, updated every year, the mystery of travel is being rapidly assassinated.

The *Athens News* series of travel books to which this volume belongs is addressed to travellers, not tourists; people who remain open to the unpredictable experiences of their travels, the inconveniences as well as the charms. Accordingly, the chapters that follow offer the reader only a minimum of practical advice, delving instead into *why* a destination is worth visiting, and leaving the reader to undertake his own adventure.

John Psaropoulos
Editor
Athens News

For Harilaos

Lake Plastiras

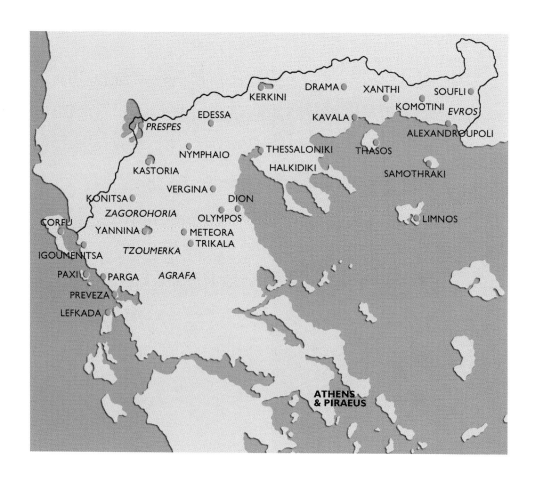

KERKINI
DRAMA
XANTHI
SOUFLI
EDESSA
KOMOTINI
EVROS
Prespes
KAVALA
ALEXANDROUPOLI
NYMPHAIO
THESSALONIKI
THASOS
KASTORIA
HALKIDIKI
SAMOTHRAKI
VERGINA
KONITSA
DION
ZAGOROHORIA
OLYMPOS
LIMNOS
CORFU
YANNINA
METEORA
IGOUMENITSA
TZOUMERKA
TRIKALA
PAXI
PARGA
AGRAFA
PREVEZA
LEFKADA
ATHENS & PIRAEUS

Table of Contents

INTRODUCTION 12

OLYMPOS TO THE WEST COAST

Olympos then and now 18

Exploring Dion 26

Getting the most out of Meteora 34

Trikala and the southern Pindos 44

Agrafa: Greece without the ruins 52

Lefkada's local colour 62

From Preveza to Igoumenitsa 70

A day in Paxi: small is beautiful 80

Paradise lost? Corfu revisited 88

EPIRUS AND NORTHERN MACEDONIA

Yannina, city on the lake — 100

The Zagorohoria revisited — 112

Exploring Tzoumerka — 126

War and peace in Konitsa — 136

Kastoria — 146

Prespes: bean kingdom on the lakes — 154

Nymphaio: rebirth of a village — 162

The Macedonian heartland: from Vergina to Edessa — 168

The allure of Thessaloniki — 178

Off the beaten track in Halkidiki — 186

EASTERN MACEDONIA AND THRACE

Lake Kerkini: a delicate balance	196
Unexpected delights in Drama	204
Kavala-Thasos: lost jewels	212
The spirit of Xanthi	222
Exploring from Xanthi	230
The coast of Thrace: from Abdera to Evros	238
Dadia's vultures and Soufli's silk	248
Didymoteicho and Komotini	254
In praise of Limnos	264
Samothraki: a goat song to the moon	274
BIBLIOGRAPHY	284

INTRODUCTION

When I crossed the border from Yugoslavia into Greece in July of 1963, it didn't occur to me to linger in the north. Despite the waves from smiling peasants homeward bound on their brightly painted carts, we headed straight for Athens and the Acropolis. I was in search of the travel poster myth – the Classical past and the romantic present evoked by a gleaming white chapel overlooking a blue abyss. The fact that Greece was also a land of evergreen forests, towering mountains, lakes and rivers, Byzantine churches and Turkish mosques would have come as a tremendous surprise.

Driving back to 'Europe' three months later, I got a taste of such northern phenomena in the improbable monasteries of Meteora, the 'Swiss' scenery around Metsovo and Yannina's lakeside silver bazaar. But even after I made Athens my home in 1972, northern Greece remained terra incognita for years. Apart from a weekend or two in Thessaloniki, treks down the Vikos gorge, up Olympos and into Agrafa, plus a few camping holidays in Thasos, Lefkada and Pelion, my unenlightened state persisted until the late 1990s.

Since then, I've been making up for lost time, trying to find out more about this other half of my adopted country. Encouraged and prodded by the *Athens News*, my husband and I have ventured east to Evros and west to Parga, north to the Prespes lakes and deep into legendary mountains — Pindos, Rhodopi, Tzoumerka and Kato Olympos. We've visited the silk town of Soufli, the fur town of Kastoria, the reborn town of Nymphaio and the watery town of Edessa. We've sighted Europe's biggest flocks of pelicans and vultures and Greece's last herd of water buffalo; we've resisted the urge to snitch wild orchid bulbs but felt no qualms about gorging on strawberries growing by the side of the road; sometimes nightingales deprived us of sleep, sometimes cuckoos timed our walks. We discovered 'unknown' antiquities at places like Amphipolis and Abdera, whose museums stunned us with their excellence, and braved the crowds at Vergina and Meteora.

Almost every meal in the north brought out the glutton in us. We learned that the fattest mussels come from Olympiada (Halkidiki), that Didymoteicho may be the sausage capital of Greece, and that Samothrace has more recipes for wild goat than the rest of the country put together. Anatolian spices flavour foods in Thrace, red peppers hot and sweet find their way into dozens of Macedonian dishes, while the *pitta* (savoury pie) reigns in Epirus. We piled the car with exquisite wines from Drama, Naoussa, Metsovo and Zitsa, and loved the fact that wherever we ate, except for Thessaloniki, we paid less than half what we would have in Athens.

The beauty and diversity of the four northern regions, Macedonia, Thrace, Epirus and Thessaly, are matched by their people. A dour face is a rarity. Invariably the locals are kind and hospitable, though impatient with Athenians' thirst for haste and frustrated with the capital getting more than its share of the budget. Eager to talk, they often have tragic stories to tell.

Memories seem to lie closer to the surface than in the south and conversations frequently turn to the Nazi occupation and the outrages of the Civil War. Occasionally they even touch on Ottoman times and the struggle for liberation. After all, unification with the south did not come until 1913 for most of the area, while the proximity and pressures of Albanians, Serbs and Bulgarians have been far more strongly felt than in Attica or the Peloponnese.

Even native Athenians feel that northern Greece is vastly different from the south. "It's not just the landscape," says a friend, "it's the people. We tend to be frivolous, light-hearted. The Macedonians and Epirots take things seriously."

But who are these northerners? Southern Greeks tend to be fairly homogeneous, but their northern compatriots come from overwhelmingly varied backgrounds. They can be Vlach shepherds or Vlach philanthropists, Pomak tobacco farmers, Turkish Thracians, Sarakatsan former nomads, refugees from Asia Minor, the Black Sea and the Caucasus, Armenians, Thesprotian Chams (Muslim Albanians), Anastenarides (Firewalkers) – Orthodox Greeks with an unorthodox way of expressing their faith – and, sadly, only tattered remnants of the Jewish communities that once thrived in Yannina, Thessaloniki, Corfu, Veria and elsewhere. Even discounting recent arrivals, the legendary Macedonian fruit salad of populations still exists even within Greek borders, never mind the Balkans as a whole. And yet most of these disparate groups consider themselves to be as Greek as any native whose roots have never been severed from his ancestors' birthplace.

In compiling this collection we drew an arbitrary line that stretches from the country's northern and eastern borders to just below Mt. Olympos, slightly downhill through Thessaly to the west coast at Preveza and into the Ionian Sea. It includes five islands but contains three notable omissions. The first, for self-evident reasons, is Mount Athos, which I could only stare at hungrily from Ouranoupolis. The second is Pelion, because we sneaked that into my earlier book *Athens and Beyond* even though it is a little far for a short weekend from the capital. The third is Metsovo.

You might well ask how a book about northern Greece could leave out such an important Macedonian landmark. And indeed it was not my intention. This enclave of Vlach initiative is one of modern Greece's success stories: a mountain town that has managed to thrive while others declined to the point of oblivion with residents numbered in single digits. Thanks to the vision of the late politician Evangelos Averoff, combined with the wealth of Baron Michael Tositsa, Metsovo's traditions have become commercially profitable. The foundation they created fosters the production of quality cheeses, wines and local crafts but it also runs two excellent museums – of folk art and modern Greek painting – as well as a ski resort, all in a dramatic setting.

Unfortunately, getting there is not half the fun. Until the completion of the Egnatia Highway that will join Thrace with Epirus, you have to slalom laboriously over the appropriately named Katara (Curse) Pass, squeezed between tourist buses and 18-wheel lorries while stifling your road rage. It was therefore all the more disappointing that, both times we made the journey recently, we found the museums shut and potential contacts at the Averoff-Tositsa Foundation off on holiday. Without this input, I felt any story could be dangerously similar to a banal brochure and so decided to postpone it for a future trip – when we inaugurate the Egnatia.

Strangely, much of northern Greece was much less off the beaten track in the past than it is today. The region was never ignored by history as Athens was from the fall of Rome to the early 19th century. Even before the original Egnatian Way linked Byzantium (later Constantinople) with Rome via Thessaloniki, trade and ideas flowed continually back and forth between east, west and north, along with disruptive armies. This means that places that are far harder to get to than Metsovo possess churches, houses, schools and art that were extraordinarily sophisticated and cosmopolitan at the time.

For example, you find semi-abandoned Epirot villages high in the Pindos mountains that exported jewellery to Paris, teachers and doctors to Moscow, and stone masons to towns all over Greece. The "builders who built the world," as these last are somewhat hyperbolically dubbed, were responsible for that quintessential northern style of architecture: stone below, plaster and half-timbering above, protruding upper stories sometimes balanced on struts, slate roofs and stained glass windows. They also perfected the arched stone bridge and the wide basilica, so different from the little square churches that dot the Peloponnese.

With so much to discover, this collection of articles – all of which were updated for this book – can do little more than help you decide where you want to go first. They are not intended to substitute for a guidebook but rather to provide some background, capture the atmosphere and draw your attention to what I found to be most intriguing about each place. We loved our explorations and hope these stories will encourage you to follow our footsteps and tyre tracks and then branch out on your own.

Many people helped me on these travels and in updating the articles. Particular thanks go to John Apgar for tips on Halkidiki, Zikos Tassios on Epirus, John and Fulla Chapple on Lefkada, Hilary Whitton Paipeti on Corfu, Elizabeth Boleman Herring on Paxi, Jonathan Tite on Agrafa, and especially Michael Cullen. Michael not only supplied many of his wonderful slides but also gave me permission to choose from his favourite hotels in places I did not have time to revisit myself. More of these can be found in his recent book, *Greece*, the latest in Alexander Sawday's series of guides to Special Places to Stay (Bristol, 2006).

PART ONE

Olympos
to the west coast

Olympos then and now

The higher one gets, the more brilliant the colours

Ag. Dionysiou (15th century), wrecked by the Nazis, now being restored

There are higher mountains in Europe, perhaps more spectacular even, but none that captures the imagination the way Olympos – or Olympus – does. It was the home of the gods after all and somehow their mystique still hovers round its peaks, lingering too in its harrowing gorges and dark fir forests. Zeus-like in its immensity, it is like Hermes in its quick-silver mutability. Sometimes the peaks are invisible behind thick clouds, sometimes they are so bright you think you can see every crevice – all in the space of a few minutes.

On this October afternoon, its vast bulk looms in every direction except up. The bald grey peaks are wreathed in fog, but the lower slopes glitter in the sunlight, a shameless extravaganza of stippled reds and golds banded by almost black evergreens. In fact Mt. Kato (Low) Olympos, only half the height of the great mountain on its eastern flank, seems more accessible and welcoming from our vantage point on the ramparts of Platamonas Castle.

This castle, superbly situated above a beach that stretches as far as the eye can see in both directions, gave its Crusader owners control over the Thermaic Gulf and the approach to Salonica. It was erected by Boniface of Montferrat, self-appointed king of Salonica after the

Zeus-like in its immensity,
Olympos was not conquered by man until 1913

The first national park in Greece, Olympos is more than cloud-covered mountain peaks: grazing, hunting, tree-cutting and even flower picking are strictly forbidden

Fourth Crusade, between 1204 and 1222 on a hill previously occupied by ancient Greeks and Byzantines. Now within its crenellated walls, it seems so peaceful that the clank of armour does not even resound in the imagination. A perfect hexagonal tower rises from a grassy knoll surrounded by peach and walnut trees; ruined chapels – some with traces of 14th cen- tury frescoes – hunker close to the fortifica- tions. But the most interesting thing about this castle today is the sudden apparition of human beings floating silently by, suspended from gleaming monowinged parachutes. Red, blue, yellow, green – there is a large flock of these ul- tramodern pterodactyls, thumbing their figura- tive noses at us grounded mortals.

Reduced to the motor vehicle, we are rewarded all the same by a spin up the slopes of Kato Olympos. Chestnut husks make deceptively soft cushions along the road and the whole mountain seems wrapped in a paisley shawl of russets, yellows and greens. Palaios Pandeleimonas and Skotina, the two villages up here, grow out of the mountain as naturally as the trees. Semi-deserted for a time, their Pelion-esque houses are being restored and the cafés and tavernas in their squares look inviting. Crimson ivy crawls up stone facades and dangles over flowerbeds crowded with marigolds and zinnias in Palaios Pandeleimonas, while in Skotina a more-than-enormous plane tree dwarfs the broad slate-roofed church next to it. Dogs lie sleeping on the rough cobbles, lulled by so much tranquillity.

Such peace and quiet is nowhere to be found in Litohoro, the gateway to Mt. Olympos itself. The town has burst its seams since I was here twenty years ago. There are new hotels, new shops – selling honey, noodles and hiking maps – and cafés by the dozen. These old-fashioned *kafeneia* are packed with men, smoking, playing cards or *tavli*, but mostly analysing election results in tones several decibels louder than normal conversation. There is not a woman in sight.

Litohoro is one of those places that prospers

Olympos's highest peak, Mytikas

from its proximity to a marvel that ranks high on many a 'must-see list'. But like the town of Delphi or Kalambaka next to Meteora, a parasitical air hovers about it. Guidebooks will tell you that it played a considerable role in the Greek struggle for independence from the Turks. They never mention that it was here that the Civil War broke out in 1946. Remembering this makes us feel even less charitable towards it.

But in the morning, watching dawn's rosy fingers splash a salmon glow over Mytikas from our hotel window, I forgive Litohoro all its shortcomings. The road up the mountain is now asphalted almost as far as Prionia, where it stops and the footpath up to Refuge A and Mytikas, the highest peak, begins. We're virtually alone on the road and the view is awesome; the mountain is so big I get a crick in my neck peering at the summits. And the higher one gets, the more brilliant the colours. Not too far up, at what must be the official entrance to the National Park, a forest worker takes our names and address and questions our destination and whether we've been here before. But despite the gloomy predictions of some trekking guides, there is still no charge for entering.

Olympos was the first area in Greece to be proclaimed a National Park. Since 1927, grazing, hunting, tree-cutting and even flower-picking are strictly forbidden. Although earlier villagers used to raise their flocks, fell trees for firewood, and hunt its wild goats, it did not occur to them to climb its peaks. This might seem strange unless you put yourself in their, rather precious, shoes. The higher reaches of the mountain offered nothing that would further their immediate livelihood. And besides, how many Greeks do you know who've never visited the Acropolis, how many New Yorkers who've never been up the Empire State Building? When you consider that the first enthusiasts to climb the Alps in the 19th century were English aristocrats, it should come as no surprise that the first men to conquer Olympos in 1913 should have been Swiss, accompanied by a local guide, of course,

Other foreigners had made attempts in the previous century. Charles Sonnini, a French naval officer, was one of the earliest, sent by Louis XVI in 1780. William Leake wandered around Kato Olympos in 1806 and an English diplomat, David Urquhart, is said to have scaled some higher peaks in 1830. In 1855 Leon Heuzey, an archaeologist, led a French mission to survey and map the mountain; German, Austrian and Serb geographers and geologists also carried out studies; and no doubt there would have been many more explorers if the area had been more peaceful. But whether under Ottoman or Greek control, the mountain was renowned for its bandits until as late as 1926. Just a year before the Swiss reached the summit, a German hiker fell into their hands and remained captive for weeks.

What made the ascent by Fred Boissonas and Daniel Ben-Bovy so memorable is that Boissonas was one of the finest photographers who ever lived. Even though he was using plates weighing more than 250 g each, he man-

Palaios Pandeleimonas grows out of the mountain as naturally as the trees

aged to take dozens of superb photos recording the adventure. He and Ben-Bovy, an art critic, both of Geneva, were also excellent writers, and had already travelled all over the Greek mainland and islands, cities and rural areas, producing albums and winning awards. Greece couldn't have asked for a better public relations campaign.

The pair had made their first visit to Greece in 1903 and were enthralled by what they saw. As Ben-Bovy wrote, "There, where others had gone seeking only ruins, we discovered a nature and a people. The archaeologists are a bit to blame, as are the art historians. They only had eyes for antiquities."

In the summer of 1913 they were on a

mission to photograph the north, from the Pindos to Thrace – areas which had just become part of Greece the previous year. They hadn't intended to tackle Olympos but an outbreak of cholera restricted their movements for a week between inoculations. They were never the types to sit still and so headed south in a kaiki.

They were lucky to meet up with Christos Kakkalos, a wood-cutter from Litohoro, who guided them up the lower peaks and the Plateau of the Muses. After a few days, they were on their way back to Litohoro when they suddenly changed their minds and decided to attempt the full ascent. On August 1st they spent the night in a woodcutter's hut and celebrated the anniversary of the founding of Switzerland in 1291. The next day they set out with Kakkalos and three other men, shepherds, who were helping with the heavy photographic equipment. But the weather turned foggy and rainy and the others dropped out. Boissonas and Ben-Bovy continued on with ropes; Kakkalos took off his shoes and scampered over the sharp rocks barefoot. As they were photographing on what they thought was the highest peak, the clouds parted and there was Mytikas. Disheartened, exhausted, but not defeated, they plodded on. Just a bit further. And they made it. The first men to conquer the highest peak in Greece, second highest in the Balkans, 2,917 m above the sea.

Since then thousands have followed in their footsteps, including yours truly. It was the 4th of July 1982, another national holiday, and the sun was shining. The walk up from Prionia to Spilios Agapitos Refuge A was not demanding, a rather gentle ascent through magical woods. There were even a few clumps of snow in the coolest recesses of the rocks. We reached the refuge in about three hours, had lunch and put our feet up, in segregated dorms. But I wasn't sleepy, the day was too fine. So I went out for a little stroll. Not far from the refuge I ran into Pericles Papamathaiou, the dear friend who was shepherding us on this adventure. "Not tired either?" he asked, "Let's go just a little further." And so it was that we found ourselves at Skala (2,866 m), ready to reach for Mytikas.

But the gods had other plans. In a twinkling of an eye, the peaks disappeared, Zeus pulled out the kettle drums, and the skies opened with buckets of ice cubes. Thunder ricocheted round the huge basin. Within minutes the mountainside was white, except for some exquisite purple flowers. The storm vanished as quickly as it had appeared. But I had had my Olympos experience and no doubts as to whether the gods were still in residence. ◯

How to get there

Platamonas and Litohoro are about four hours' drive north on the Athens-Thessaloniki National Road; about 1½ hours from Thessaloniki, depending on the traffic. You can also take the train or intercity bus to Litohoro.

Where to stay

Litohoro has dozens of hotels, none of them terribly distinguished but quite adequate. In Palaios Panteleimonas, the *Pliades hotel*, a traditional building on the outskirts of the village (23520 22661), has a spectacular view of the sea and the peaks. It was about to renovated in 2005 and its manager, Takis Parashos, was hoping to finish before Christmas. If you are feeling more adventurous, Nikos Karagiannidis takes people trekking on Olympos, as well as canyoning and cross-country skiing, from his base at Ano Skotina, about 15 km higher. Groups of friends can rent his stone house in this deserted but lovely hamlet and he's building a second next door, which will have three apartments. Call him at 6973 220888 for details.

To climb Mt. Olympos

There are many routes to the various peaks; the path most taken is from Prionia to Refuge A Spilios Agapitos and from there to Mytikas. The refuge is open from May 15 to October 31, and you can book one of the 80 beds by calling 23520 81800. Several hiker's guides exist, which can give you maps and detailed information about paths and refuges. *The Mountains of Greece* by Tim Salmon with Michael Cullen, a Cicerone guide, is the most up to date.

Where to eat

There are promising tavernas under the trees in the heart of Palaios Panteleimonas, while *Pliades* has the best view and the best chef, who turns out local specialities as well as the usual grilled meats. Otherwise, try the bean soup and other simple fare at the *Stavros Refuge* (23510 84100) and the taverna at Prionia in summer. Meals are also available at *Spilios Agapitos Refuge*.

Whether you ever climb Olympos or not, a new album of Boissonas' photos and texts by him, Ben-Bovy and other climbers was published in Greek (2002) by the Municipality of Litohoro. Even if you don't read Greek, the photos need no translation.

Exploring Dion

> The first sanctuary
> proved to be a hybrid
> dedicated first to Artemis
> Eilithya, goddess
> of childbirth, and later
> to Isis.

It was a gorgeous Friday, sunny, not too hot, and we were even looking forward to the long drive north. The traffic was light, to the point that somewhere after Lamia, we started wondering where everyone was. At Pelasgia, joining a barrage of trucks backed up for miles, we found out. We grumbled there for another 40 minutes. The only vehicles in motion were the occasional "me-firsters" who would skid off into the wrong lane and sprint down the formidable wall of 18-wheelers to the head of the line. Irate drivers splayed their fingers in the well known Greek version of "up yours", shouting vociferously from their exalted cabins. The game continued sporadically until the driver of a shiny milk tanker, too irritated for words, suddenly lunged his huge vehicle into the path of a sneaky sedan. Teamster and smart-ass exchanged insults for five minutes before the sedan escaped off the tarmac up to the top of the hill. This version of road rage à la grecque effectively put an end to other would-be queue jumpers, who had to content themselves with mere muttering.

Once we got moving again – after dump trucks cleared away a bit of blasted mountainside – the driving really became unpleasant. From Pelasgia to Tempi we were funnelled into a diabolical treadmill of bewildering blue YES arrows, unyielding red NO banners, shifting widths, single lanes with two-way traffic, double lanes with one-way traffic, no way to tell the difference, plus dust clouds, the roar of heavy machinery and the spectacle of injured, bruised landscape being slowly turned into highway. Every now and then we'd halt within sight of a mangled wreck and think of those all too repetitive weekend statistics. One day, many years in the future, the face of Greece will be changed by modern road networks. Intercity travel will be a breeze, but for now driving requires infinite patience and nerves of steel.*

By the time we saw the signs for the archaeological site and museum of Dion, we were more than ready for a break. Like so many signposted places in Greece, the actual location of this major

Unknown goddesses lost among the reeds

sanctuary to Olympian Zeus is left for you to intuit, so when we reached a crossroads near the hamlet of Platanakia, we instinctively followed a series of incongruous four-globed street lights planted along the country lane. The site itself is marked by a modern glass building, where you buy your ticket and can pick up the excellent illustrated guidebook by Dimitrios Pandermalis, its chief archaeologist for more than thirty years. *(NB: Signage was much improved by 2005.)*

The huge area, bisected by a road and a river, resembles an untended golf course more than a swanky Macedonian-Roman town. And a golf cart would come in handy because the buildings that have been excavated are sparse and far apart. But this spaciousness is part of its appeal.

Though connected from early antiquity with the cults of the Muses, Orpheus and Dionysos, Dion was first and foremost linked with the worship of Zeus for whom it was named. *Dios* (mod. *Dias*) is the genitive form of the name and comes from the same Sanskrit root as the Latin *deus*, meaning god. The Macedonians, followed by the Romans, gathered there for games and

Statues once stood on these bases near the baths

rituals; a town grew up to serve pilgrims and eventually also accommodated Christians, whose churches stood next to pagan temples. Sometime during the 5th century AD, earthquakes and floods forced the inhabitants to evacuate and the buildings gradually sank into what became a vast marsh, sealing its secrets from plunderers and scholars. In Dion's prime, though, the river was navigable and allowed the sanctuary to become one of the largest spas in the country.

We ambled along a cobbled path and across the road to what is left of the so-called Great Roman baths, the most magnificent of the ten bath complexes found at Dion, which was spread over 4,000 sq. m. Here, advanced plumbing provided hot, tepid and cold water, as well as synergistic public loos – a marble bench with holes directly over a sewage channel flushed by waste water from the baths. Apparently the Romans dubbed toilets of this kind Vespasianae after the emperor who had the temerity to tax them, making "spending a penny" seem a bargain. But a bath was more than a place to soak in those days and they combined all the functions of a gym, café, concert hall and shrine – the original multiplex centre. They were also lavishly decorated. Statuary, portraits of local dignitaries and benefactors, as well as of gods and goddesses, filled the corners and niches and all the floors were paved with mosaics. The statues have been moved to the museum, but many of the mosaics are still in place.

Be warned, though. Between the end of October and Easter, they are concealed under plastic sheeting covered with a thick layer of sand. It would be a shame to miss them because the Dion mosaics represent the pinnacle of the art. In delicate beiges, creams and greys, one shows a sensuous O'Keefe-esque flower, another, an exquisite droopy-eyed bull. Those in the so-called villa of Dionysos are the most stunning of all: they depict the god in a chariot drawn over the waves by sea panthers reined in by sea centaurs, framed by masks of satyrs and curly-locked women and surrounded by an intricate garland of gold leaves and tendrils on a black background. Incredibly sophisticated and covering 100 sq. m, this was the flooring for a 2nd century AD banquet hall. Sadly, it is too well protected by a shed surrounded by wire netting to be truly appreciated, so buy a postcard.

A broad Roman highway leads to the other major sight in this part of Dion, a large Early Christian basilica. It too boasts mosaics and was the first building in the ancient town to be excavated. By sheer coincidence, the archaeologist, George Sotiriadis of the University of Thessaloniki, was my first husband's grandfather. In 1928 this distinguished man started a three year search for Zeus's sanctuary, which he knew had to be there, in the foothills of the sacred mountain. Contemporary accounts had told of Philip II thanking the god at Dion after his victories in northern Greece, of Alexander praying for his help before setting out for Persia and, more than a hundred years earlier, of Archelaos erecting a temple to Zeus, a stadium (for the Macedonian Olympics), and a theatre where Euripides' plays drew crowds. Poor Pappou – he died long before I came to Greece – battled swamp fever, hordes of vampire-like mosquitoes and appallingly primitive conditions only to find a ruin some six centuries newer than what he sought.

One more summer would have rewarded him. Decades later, in 1964, when the university resumed excavating, another archaeologist, G. Bakalakis, dug just a few centimetres deeper and found the ancient walls and the Roman theatre. But it was left to Dimitrios Pandermalis, his successor, to uncover the shrines, the baths and the magnificent villa. He has devoted more than thirty years to the site and has performed Herculean tasks like diverting the river and slogging through eight metres of mud in order to reach

The original multiplex: one of the so-called Great Roman baths, providing the functions of gym, café, concert hall and shrine

temple foundations. The first sanctuary he tackled proved to be a hybrid dedicated first to Artemis Eilithya, goddess of childbirth, and later to Isis, an Egyptian deity imported after Alexander's successes in the Middle East. The goddess was worshipped in various capacities – as a protectress of women during and after childbirth but also as Isis Tyche, bringer of good fortune. The charming niches and pools in her sanctuary, where statue replicas glow through thick clumps of reeds, are even now very boggy with raucous frogs and brilliant blue dragonflies, the goddess's

only worshippers. This small, intimate shrine, so unlike the formal Doric temples we are used to, must have been soothing to worried women supplicants. Today it brings grins of delight.

Wandering round the park-like site some more was good for the constitution but less exciting archaeologically. The actual shrine to Zeus is still under excavation and there are only two rows of original seats in the Hellenistic theatre, though it has been equipped with a full complement of wooden ones for summer festival performances. Drama erupted from another source, however, when two very belligerent geese left the flock that has taken up residence near the pond by the refreshment area and started lunging provocatively at our backsides.

We found refuge in the museum, a few blocks away. There are so many statues assembled in the main room that one can easily imagine how crowded the baths must have been even without the presence of all those toga-less Romans. Some torsos and heads positively gleam after their long burial in the mud; if a mud bath is considered a tonic for human skin, it certainly works wonders for marble, though it is true that others wear an amber stain. Almost all the sculptures are Hellenistic and Roman. Purists may argue that they are fussier than those of the Classical or Archaic periods, but here they seem compellingly human, even moving. Not only are there whole families of the immortals – Asklepios and his sons and daughters taken from the baths, Isis/Aphrodite/Artemis and Demeter in various guises – but many portrait busts of men and women so sensitively executed you feel you know them. The latest find, a statue of Zeus Ypsistos (Most High) that turned up in 2003, stands roped off, but all the others are very approachable and slightly smaller than life-size. Another exhibit had me mystified in 1998: several sets of footprints carved into marble plaques, rather like the hands of movie stars pressed into

the cement outside Graumann's Chinese Theater in Hollywood. But they didn't even match. These have since been moved to the sanctuary of Isis and were a form of votive offering to her.

The most intriguing thing on display at Dion is the oldest pipe organ in the world, and one of only two in existence. Pandermalis extricated its green-patinated, bronze pipes from the mud in 1992. Invented by an Alexandrian engineer in the 3rd century BC, the hydraulis gradually evolved into the mighty ecclesiastical organ that can span two stories. As its name implies, this metre-high 1st century BC model used air pumped through water to produce its notes, but we'll have to imagine what they sounded like. I like to think of the organist playing an aubade for the bathers with the frogs and geese contributing the accompaniment. ⭕

---

* The National Road has improved a good deal since this article was first published in the spring of 1998. I included this description as a reminder of what we faced then and how much has been accomplished. Alas, a few problem areas still exist, most notably between Theologos-Agios Konstantinos-Ahinos (near Stylida) – the notorious Malliakos "horseshoe", where traffic is squeezed into one lane on a single carriageway and the most fatal accidents have occurred.

How to get there

Dion lies about 10 minutes off the National Road, between Katerini and Litohoro.

Where to stay

There are plenty of hotels at Litohoro but the *Pliades* in Pal. Panteleimonas would be my choice (see p. 25).

Where to eat

A row of pleasant looking tavernas faces the museum but I cannot vouch for them.

In spring frogs love Dion's pools

Getting the most out of Meteora

This is a place that has
to be seen to be believed,
like the Taj Mahal or the
Grand Canyon.

When Eric Newby and his wife Wanda rolled into Meteora in 1983 to gather research and anecdotes for inclusion in *On the Shores of the Mediterranean*, they were so dismayed by the crowds, coaches and "phalanxes of motorcycles" that they cut their visit short and high-tailed it off to Mt. Olympos. Their expectations having been fired by stomach-churning accounts of ascents in frayed rope-sacks by Robert Curzon in the early 19th century and by Patrick Leigh Fermor's romantic evocation of post-war decline and decay, they felt they had arrived "at least twenty years too late." Nevertheless, a score or so years later still, the insane landscape and the monasteries of the air do work their magic, despite the hordes – if you know how to approach them.

Miraculously crowned on the tops of 24 pinnacles, no reproduction can convey the amazement one feels faced with the monasteries

After the long drive through the com and wheat fields of the Thessaly plain, the great grey rocks of the Meteora surging from it like the legs of a bodyless behemoth come as a shock no matter how much you've read, how many photos you've looked at. This is a place that has to be seen to be believed, like the Taj Mahal or the Grand Canyon. No reproduction can convey the amazement or emotion one feels faced with the genuine article. And nothing can dull that first impression, not even the banality of Kalambaka or the strings of campsites and dilapidated discos that line the road up to this dreary little town. For Kalambaka is a leach like Delphi; its only reason for existence is to shelter, feed and sell souvenirs to the tourists who throng to its spectacular sites and monuments. Add to that the fact that in 1945, as Leigh Fermor writes, it was "just a ramshackle collection of temporary wooden huts standing in a circle of blackened hearths and shattered chimney stacks," and you understand, even sympathise, with its utter lack of pretence.

But commiseration does not constitute a reason for staying there. A truly charming alternative lies just a couple of kilometres up the road. In Kastraki not only will you find a village atmosphere and even a cluster of prewar buildings but you'll be closer to the mighty rocks. In the early morning and at twilight when fewer people are about, the stillness and solemnity of their almost overpowering presence can impress itself upon you without distractions.

Or so I thought one morning in May when, desperate to commune with the startling pinnacles on my own, I struck out on foot for "Old Kastraki" and branched off onto a path that seemed to lead to a neglected white chapel. From there it disappeared into a glade where dozens of birds screeched and trilled and sunlight splattered onto ferns and mossy stones. I padded soundlessly along the trail, poked my nose into another rickety church and sang a hymn of praise under my breath in homage to whatever deity had a part in this blissful side trip. Then I began to be aware of another kind of screeching in a language not yet recognizable but definitely human. I kept walking in the direction of the sounds, slightly apprehensive but curious, and before long I was out of the woods on a slope from which a smallish but still awesome spike protruded like a narwhal's tusk. I saw the source of the shouts – a foursome of German women – and their menfolk, two of them waving from the tip of the tusk while the third helped the fourth scale the last few feet of nubbly rockface and scramble onto the top. I blanched and felt my toes curl but could not take my eyes off the men, who looked like Gullivers among the Brobdinagians, mice attacking

Truly suspended between heaven and earth

Even without the monasteries, there is something spiritual about the Meteora

a gigantosaur. I stayed there mesmerised until all four had come swinging down on red and blue ropes, twirling with perfect aplomb, one so adept he was barefoot.

How the need for excitement, pitting ourselves against nature, pushes us to ever greater feats! (At least some of us – I'd rather watch.)

For centuries monks and the odd visitor were hauled up to their eyries and back down again with ropes. It was either that or test the rungs of a series of rickety ladders dangling hundreds of feet above the void. Since the early 1930s steep steps have replaced them. Access to the monasteries may be hard on the knees or the lungs but is otherwise not dangerous. Now the thrill is gone but the rocks still exert their challenge. Like Everest, they are there, so climbing them is an increasingly popular sport.

To find out more about it, I traipsed after the Germans to the Camping Vrahos, a ten-minute walk away, where I'd heard there was an English-speaking rock-climbing school. "And so there is," the owner assured me, "but it hasn't opened yet. Perhaps instead you'd like to talk to the man who teaches gliding; he knows about climbing, too."

I couldn't believe my ears. It was said that Saint Athanasios, who founded the Great Meteoron, the earliest, largest and highest of the monasteries at some 600 m above sea level, had flown up to the rock of his choice on the back of an eagle. And in fact no one has been able to come up with a more plausible theory, let alone explain how he and his followers constructed such amazing edifices. But now people were soaring around them – every age has its secrets, unfathomable to the uninitiated.

Later that evening, Chris du Bois, a French-

Viewed from above,
the rock formations
resemble a bodyless
behemoth

born citizen of the world, told me how safe tandem paragliding is: "100 percent and it's not scary either, though you need time to relax, talk to the teacher, drive yourself a bit, and look around. We fly from the plateau near Agios Stephanos monastery, for about 20 minutes, which is just right for the first time."

Chris became poetic as he described the wonders that he'd discovered while plotting hikes and climbs for people: "Anyone can climb. If you believe in your leader and if you really want to, you can get over your fears. I love the rewards – deserted monasteries where there are no buses, no tourists, no monks; the rivers, the forests, the flowers and, best of all, a night spent sleeping on the rocks. That's when you really feel the power and the spirit of the place."

The Meteora he had found must be not unlike the refuge sought by the legions of monks and hermits who began to flock here as early as the 10th century. Athanasios himself arrived in 1336 from Mount Athos and was soon joined by dozens of others. By the 16th century they had seemingly miraculously crowned the tops of twenty-four pinnacles with monasteries and hermitages and, as one old-timer told Leigh Fermor, there was "a hermit in every hole in the rocks, like hives full of bees." The monasteries flourished, supported at first by Serbian kings and Byzantine emperors who granted them estates in such farflung places as Wallachia and Moldavia as well as Thessaly. Once established in Greece, the Ottomans respected their property and gave them further privileges, but, ironically, it was peace and the birth of the new Greek state that hastened their desertion, eliminating the need for their traditional role as a bastion of nationalism and repository of Greek culture. Ironically, too, their sanctity remained unviolated by any invaders until the middle of the 20th century, when, first, German shells damaged some of their buildings and then, some twenty years later, they opened their gates to mass tourism and, for the most part, gave up their monastic function in order to operate as museums.

In the six monasteries that are still inhabited, the spiritual component is noticeable in its absence. I detected it in only two, the smallest, Agios Nikolaos Anapafsa, where there were but two monks, and Agios Stephanos, now a nunnery with young, sweet-faced sisters whose serenity contrasted refreshingly with the brisk "sergeant-majors" sullenly directing traffic at the other convent, Roussanou. Agios Nikolaos also has the finest frescoes, painted by the famous 16th century Cretan hagiographer, Theophanes. Agios Stephanos has the most recent. Its main church was rebuilt after the war and its walls were in the process of being repainted, offering an opportunity to watch fresco artists in action on their scaffolding.

To enjoy the other monasteries – Metamorphosis or Great Meteoron, Barlaam (Varlaam), Roussanou (also called Agia Varvara), and Agios Triados – try to be there when they open at 9 am or in the afternoon before they shut at 6 pm. (Some also close between 1 and 3.30, and each has a different day of rest.) To avoid the saturation that comes with looking at too many scenes of bone-chilling martyrdom – monsters with kicking limbs sprouting from their toothy maws, saints on the rack, being flagellated, speared, roasted, beheaded – and a surfeit of intricately crafted ecclesiastical treasures, do not attempt to "do" more than two monasteries in one day. Even the exotic palls when one is too well fed. But be sure to spend several moments in contemplation of the old rope bag and primitive pulley at Varlaam, where the abbot only changed the rope "when it broke," and then go off somewhere by yourself or with a paragliding or rock-climbing instructor from Vrahos Camping and give the surreal scenery of the Meteora a chance to impart its mysteries to you. ◯

How to get there

Situated in Central Greece between the Pindos mountains and the plain of Thessaly, Meteora can be reached by bus or train from Athens to Larissa (4 hours on the intercity express train), where there are frequent bus and train connections to Kalambaka (2 hours). Kastraki is a twenty-minute walk or short taxi ride from Kalambaka station. You can hike, hitch or hire a cab to take you to the monasteries.

Where to stay (area code 24320)

In addition to the dozens upon dozens of rooms and hotels in Kastraki and Kalambaka, there are at least three exceptional, moderately priced hotels where the atmosphere is all you could hope for and the owners helpful and friendly: *Hotel Meteora* (22367, in Kalambaka), *Doupiani House* (75326), *Hotel Kastraki* (75336). Two Campsites, both with pools, are also far above average: *Camping Boufidis/The Cave* is superbly situated just below Agios Nikolaos Anapafsa, while the expanded *Camping Vrahos* (22293), hosts the Climb a Rock school, now run by No Limits. You don't have to stay there to take part.

Where to eat

The locals recommend the following tavernas: *Gardhenia* on the main square, *Philoxenia*, and *Stelios* in Kastraki and, in Kalambaka, *Koka Roka*, in the upper town, and *Gertsos/The Meteora* on the second square (*defteri plateia*). At *To Tzaki*, on the main road between Kalambaka and Yannina, the speciality is meat grilled in the fireplace.

This piece appeared in the *Athens News* on 8 August 1997. Alas, gliding from the rocks is no longer offered, but a talk with Lazaros Botelis, head of the climbing school, almost made me want to scale the pinnacles.

"Of course, you could do it," he said, "all you really need is to bolster your confidence and within two or three days, you could be tackling almost any rock. We offer lessons for all ages and levels of experience and supply all the equipment, including the boots. The technology is so advanced now, you have no fear of falling, and your leader never takes more than two people under him. Why don't you come try it in off-season? Spring and fall are particularly beautiful and we're open all year."

No Limits also organizes rafting in the rivers around Grevena, 50 minutes' drive away. Call 24320 79165 for further information.

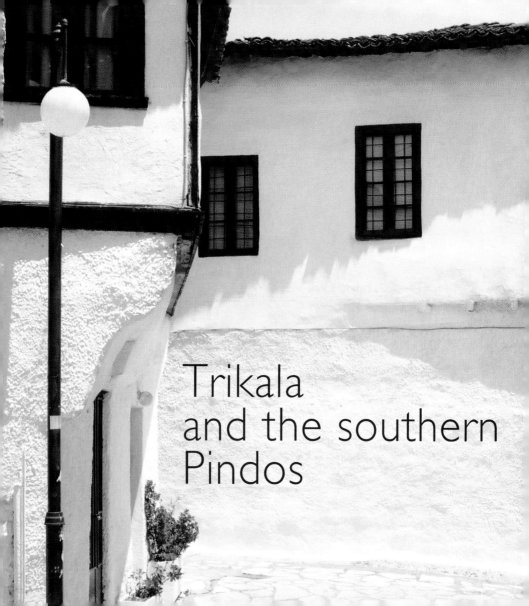

Trikala
and the southern
Pindos

Until a decade ago known only to goatherds, loggers and partisans, the southern Pindos has become a weekend resort for urbanites. Boutique hotels have taken the place of cowsheds.

I n the summer of 1997, the year the *Athens News* started my travel stories, I reported on a velvet revolution taking place in Volos, Larissa and Trikala, the traditionally scorned cities of the great plain of Thessaly. "Secretly, quietly, without any fuss or fanfare, [they] are transforming themselves into cities with charm, where it's a pleasure to spend some time instead of passing through with eyes squeezed shut and nose in the air.

"It's not easy for a town to rise above its location if it happens to be anywhere near a plain. We tend to assume flat equals drab equals grain equals tractors, dust and just 'plain' boring. The plain of Thessaly, Greece's breadbasket, seems to loom as a big yawn on our way to Meteora, Olympos or Pelion since we are not looking at it with a conqueror's covetous gleam or a historian's curiosity."

In the past, the three towns were dismissed in most guidebooks with such telegraphic descriptions as "a transportation hub", "there is no reason to prolong your stay", "gives no hint of its ancient past", and the like. Damning with faint praise, Osbert Lancaster wrote, "Trikkala alone, by the possession of a Turkish castle and a couple of dilapidated mosques, achieves some faint character of its own." But he'd have to eat his words now. In all three cities dust has given way to greenery, traffic-clogged streets to pedestrian precincts, kafeneia where old men play cards to "cafeterias" where the young sip frappés under designer umbrellas. And Trikala's faint character has not been lost in the transition but rather nurtured by judicious restorations in its old district.

In 2005, I returned to what Patrick Leigh Fermor called "the dusty lowland town by the winding Peneios" and discovered that while Trikala continues to be full of new life, a second

The back streets of Varosi, Trikala's old district, re a warren of white houses and stone chambers revolution is quietly changing its hinterland, the southern Pindos. That verdant region, until a decade ago known only to goatherds, loggers and partisans, has become a weekend resort for urbanites desperate for clean air and wood-burning fireplaces. Boutique hotels have taken the place of cowsheds.

Trikala

There are two Trikalas in Greece. The collection of villages in the mountains of Korinthia is so called because of 'their three good things' – water, soil and climate. The city on the north-west edge of the plain of Thessaly could never brag about its climate. Instead, its name reflects its long ago existence as Trikke, which Homer mentioned as sending soldiers to Troy. The extra 'k' fell by the wayside in the last twenty years, a victim to spelling reforms.

No signs direct you to ancient Trikke for the simple reason that continuous habitation has wiped out all trace of what was reputed to be the birthplace of Asklepios, the god of medicine. Nothing remains but some fine building blocks recycled in a few of the churches scattered through the oldest part of town and a scruffy pile of stones thought to be the god's first hospital.

It's even harder to picture Trikala as the

There was not a hotel room to be found in Elati due to the annual visit of the Sarakatsan tribes

centre of a Bulgarian-Vlach kingdom called Great Wallachia in the 12th century or as the seat of Serb ruler Stephen Dusan's Kingdom of Thessaly in 1345. As Lancaster implied, the most picturesque parts of Trikala are Turkish.

During the almost five hundred years of Ottoman occupation, Trikala was the provincial capital of Thessaly. The huge main mosque, Kursum Tsami, beneficiary of a recent facelift, stands by itself on the outskirts of town. But as the city's website proudly boasts, Trikala has "many beauties… enough sights and saves many smartly mansions" (sic). These are to be found in the old quarter, Varosi, a warren of white houses with projecting upper floors, funky shops, ouzeris and those 16th and 17th century churches with the purloined Classical masonry. Above them a mouldering castle wall interrupts a surprisingly wooded hill with staccato bursts of Morse code in stone.

Hoping for a prowl round the fortress, which Byzantines constructed over the ancient acropolis, we slogged up the path in the June sun. There, instead of the castle proper, closed to the public, we were offered a thirties era castelletto/café set amidst a shady park with serpentine pools. A long drink in this popular trysting spot revived us sufficiently to appreciate the view of the river as it undulated through town.

It's not the Pineios, but rather a tree-lined branch of it called the Lithaios (no relation to ancient Lethe). Ten bridges, only half of them for cars, shunt traffic back and forth between the trendy hangouts around the two main squares on either side of the river. Trikala's heart, however, is the immense boulevard, Asklepiou, which leads up to them and is for people only. This precinct is dedicated to the swish café, and its youthful customers seem even more intent in keeping up with current fashions than their peers in Kolonaki or Kypseli. Bared navels have long since taken the place of the *tseberi* (head scarf), while ads for gyms and martial arts schools indicate that ploughing fields no longer counts as a primary mode of exercise. This is the new Trikala, lively and attractive, still fuelled by agriculture but by no means stuck in a furrow.

Into the southern Pindos

Just a few miles to the southwest of the Trikala wheat fields, there begins a land of thick forests, clear rivers and lush pastures ringed by overlapping green mountains. It's the kind of idealised Swiss landscape you find in Hallmark Christmas cards. The little travelled loop that runs from Pyli, 30 km from Trikala, to Mourgani, 10 km north of flat Kalambaka, gets no mention in most guides. It boasts not one archaeological site and just a few distinctive churches.

The first, Porta Panayia at Pyli, is so called because it marks the gateway to the gorge that leads into the southern Pindos. Consecrated in 1283, this unusual church was plonked right on top of a temple to Athena or Apollo. Its builders made good use of the marble, which they combined with exceptional decorative brickwork. In the vicinity, the 16th century monastery of Agios Vissarionos Dousikas is said to be equally eye-catching but bars its doors to females.

The main attraction in this area is the small

A land of thick forests, clear rivers and lush pastures exists just a few miles
beyond the Trikala wheat fields

ski resort at Pertouli. Since its opening, hotels of all kinds have been swelling villages and tempting city slickers deeper into the wilderness. Being lower, Elati, whose very name means fir tree, is more developed, but despite its many rooms, we couldn't find a bed. Everything was booked for the annual meeting of the Sarakatsan tribes from the four corners of northern Greece. Posters in shop windows described the three-day programme, which seemed to consist mainly of dancing and feasting at the plateau where the ski lifts start.

I had to be content with a small display of rainbow-hued Sarakatsan costumes in Elati's Fretzato hotel. Its owner told me that some 25,000 of these mysterious, once nomadic people would be gathering and while this sounded like a wild exaggeration, it made me long to be a witness. So next year you know where I'll be on the third weekend in June.

This being Thursday, we did find a room at Pertouli, a magnificent room with wood-panelled cupboards and ceiling, a down duvet (still needed), damask curtains that matched the slipcovers on cushy armchairs in a hotel that looked like an elegant country club. Given the price, we were not surprised to be the only guests and the only diners in the (excellent) baronial restaurant.

Dimitris Poulios, who runs the Arhontiko Hatzigaki, treated us like visiting royalty and gave us a tour of its buildings. Owned by a prominent Trikala family which has spawned many a politician, the mansion went up in 1890. In the 40s, the Communists made it their local headquarters but destroyed it when they retreated. Only the walls remained until the early 1990s when Dimitris Hatzigakis, brother of the ND MP and a civil engineer, set about rebuilding it exactly as it had been. It took him seven years.

The miracle is how well he succeeded. Absolutely all the woodwork – including ceilings, doors, staircases and floors – looks crafted by master carpenters a hundred years ago. How wonderfully reassuring to know that such artisans still exist. However, this is no Victorian period piece. The rest of the décor can be classified as 'elegant rustic', comfortable but not fussy or prim.

In the morning after inspecting the grounds – mostly lawn and giant trees – on a hillock above the entrance to Pertouli, I walked down to the village. There, a trio of women had taken over the parking space next to their home/taverna and were spreading something that looked like coarse sand over linen sheets laid out on a row of bed frames. They beckoned to me to help myself from tubs of black cherries that were soon to become spoon sweets and told me they were drying *trahana*. Women have been storing these minute pellets of crushed wheat boiled with sheep's milk since time immemorial; *trahana* (sometimes also made with flour) may even be the first pasta.

As we drove higher into the mountain, we passed more villages that looked exactly like Pertouli. Clusters of little white houses roofed with red tin, plus a few freaks on stilts, their charm grows with distance. But it's not their fault. Nazis or Communist guerrillas burnt the original villages in the hate-filled 1940s.

Any scars are invisible. The scenery is a banquet for the eyes, the roadside a botanical garden. Stopping the car to photograph a colony of pink orchids, I was soon feasting on wild strawberries. We inched our way north, wishing we had time to hike through the woods or bounce down the river in a kayak.

We hadn't seen a village in miles when all of

a sudden, near Kalliroi, an apparition loomed into view. Called Pyrgos (Chateau) Mantania, it looked far too grand for the area but was actually modelled on local mansions destroyed in the war. Two massive grey-stone wings opening onto a paved court contrasted starkly with the lush green surroundings, but the interior was cosy, welcoming and full of colour. The rustic lounge alone had fuchsia walls, old floor tiles and a cornflower-blue wooden ceiling, which sounds garish but wasn't. The bedrooms were light and airy, with pastel walls and fireplaces.

The place was empty except for Yorgos, the cook doubling as receptionist. He said the hotel opened in October 2002 and filled up every weekend, even though it's a good six hours from Athens. People come because the Pyrgos offers so many activities: treks or drives in 4x4 jeeps to the source of the Acheloos river high in the mountains or to 'the' waterfall, stone bridges and monasteries. I'd love to return in May for their mushroom-gathering seminar.

But, being in a rush this time, the only sight we managed was the amazing church at Doliana a few kilometres further. Built of the same stone as the Chateau, its dozen turrets and nine apses swell from the sides and roof, giving an impression of continuous movement. Medieval looking plaques with low reliefs of big-eyed angels, the two-headed eagle and crosses rising from the

tails of geese(?) decorate the windowless walls, but they are really 18th century naif.

When we arrived, the young guard was waiting for the locksmith. Burglars had attempted to break in the previous day and had jammed the lock. "They can't have been from around here. Everyone knows there's nothing left to steal."

The locksmiths told us the whole story. It seems the church was the scene of a series of massacres in 1943. Both the partisans and the Nazis had taken prisoners. An exchange of prisoners fell through, and the *antartes* took their 76 captives to the church and murdered them. In retaliation, the Nazis went on a rampage, killing not only their prisoners but hundreds of other villagers, whom they chased into the forest, burning their homes as well. Everyone died except twin boys who were found two days later still suckling at their mother's breast.

"And then, after the war, in 1960, the Germans came back and stole all our icons," said the older locksmith. I wondered what proof he had but the fact remains, the interior is decorated by new icons that shine too brightly amidst the forest of stone columns that support the domes.

It was a lesson. History simmers under the surface in Greece, even where it is most beautiful. ○

How to get there

Trikala lies due west of Larissa, but from Athens it is safer and quicker to drive via Lamia and Karditsa. You can easily combine a visit to the southern Pindos with a trip to Meteora, just 33 km from Trikala. A stunning circular route would start with Pyli, 30 km southwest of Trikala, Elati, Pertouli, Kalliroi and Kastania to Mourgani, where you rejoin the main Metsovo-Kalambaka-Trikala road. All the surfaces are tarmacked.

Arhontiko Hatzigaki

Where to stay

In Trikala, the B class *Divani* (24310 27286) or the C class *Lithaion* (24310 20690).
Pyrgos Mantania, Kalliroi Aspropotamou, 16 rooms, cosy living room with fireplace (24320 87351/87600), www.mantania-ae.gr
Arhontiko Hatzigaki, Pertouli, 23 rooms, several common rooms, fireplaces, and games rooms (24340 91146-9).
Fretzato, Elati, 10 rooms in the middle of town (24340 71872), www.fretzato.gr

Where to eat

Both the *Pyrgos Mantania* and *Arhontiko Hatzigaki* have their own restaurants. In Trikala, Ypsilantou pedestrian street might better be called *Taverna Alley*.

Agrafa:
Greece without the ruins

It seems a land barely lapped by the main stream of history, a place for hardy shepherds, woodcutters, subsistence farmers, and nowadays for nature-worshippers.

The man in front of me stopped short, nostrils quivering like a retriever on point. In an instant, the fragrance stunned me too and simultaneously we fell to our knees and began plucking tiny ruby-red nuggets from the side of the path. Almost swooning with their perfume, we gobbled delectable handfuls. It's not often one comes across a bed of wild strawberries in one's wanderings. But the Agrafa is full of such surprises and unexpected treats.

The serrated peaks of Panaitoliko

The summit of Mt Borlero one snowy April, looking south past the peaks of Flidzani (2016m) towards distant Mt Timfristos (Velouhi).

This is the "unwritten" region of Greece, the blank space on the map between Thessaly and Epirus, which was too wild for the Turkish census takers and virtually everyone else before or since. There are no Doric columns rising alongside the fir trees, no shrines to Demeter or Herakles, no memories of visits by Alexander, Nero or a Palaiologos emperor. It seems a land barely lapped by the main stream of history, a place for hardy shepherds, woodcutters, subsistence farmers, and nowadays for nature-worshippers.

When I first arrived in Athens in the early 70s, the occasional friend would mention the Agrafa as a fascinating but extremely remote area whose few inhabitants were in dire need of blankets and old clothes. A couple of acquaintances had even camped on the outskirts and returned with tales of extreme beauty and total serenity. Over the years we'd talk about setting out like Pooh on an "expotition" to this southernmost extension of the Pindos, but somehow I never imagined it would ever happen. Nevertheless, here we were, springing along mossy paths, swimming in torrents, teetering on ridges, and nursing our blisters.

Trekking Hellas made it possible, with its bi- (even tri-) lingual guides whose warm, friendly nature charms both locals and tenderfeet, and its deceptively laid-back organisation, which arranged for the tiled shower and flushing loo in our quarters in Agrafa village, one of the very first in the region. They ferried us to the best hiking spots, cutting out the gruelling and the dull, relieved us of our rucksacks, and supplied us with botanical, geographical and folkloric titbits that kept us nourished long after we'd devoured our picnic.

Making our way from Karpenissi into the heart of this wilderness required snaking up miles of red dirt hairpin bends, crossing new concrete

A peripatetic barber attracts his regular clients in Vrangiana

bridges erected alongside Indiana Jones-type slatted relics that looked ready to collapse. We laboured in second gear through oak forests, plane tree groves, pine woods and firs with pale green "candles" of fresh growth on the tips of their branches, without glimpsing a single settlement. Raw bulldozed slashes showed evidence of road building, but there was no sign of what they might be linking until the umpteenth curve brought us in sight of Agrafa village amidst the chestnut and walnut trees.

With some 250 inhabitants it is the largest conglomeration of people in the district, which has lost much of its population in recent years.

A cheerful collection of red-roofed stone houses was loosely grouped around a slate-topped
church coiffed with a chef's hat cupola. Its paths
were awash with burbling streams and red roses ran riot everywhere. We became friends
with Niki Komboyanni, who cooked for us and
discussed her varicose veins with my surgeon
husband. You would never travel to Agrafa for
the cuisine but her "real" fried potatoes, lamb
stews, meatballs and salads tasted exquisite after a day in the mountains, though the *retsina*
scorched the throat… at first. The old boys
smacking their lips over *tsipouro* poured liberal-
ly from a Cutty Sark bottle had no doubt found
a better beverage.

Our late June evenings were cool, jolly, lit by
fireflies and serenaded by nightingales, but it
was the days that were truly magical. Hours of
fairly strenuous climbing along a treeless slope
would be rewarded with extraordinary views –
of nearly all the mountains in central Greece
from Smolika to Parnassos, some snow-capped,
some as jagged as a shark's tooth, some napped

Guarded by the peaks of the eastern Agrafa, the manmade lake Plastiras
provides hydroelectric power and irrigation

with green or ribbed with grey scree. Now and again we'd glimpse a lake, Kremaston to the south, milky blue Plastiras to the north. Our sightings of wildlife ranged from the sublime to the ridiculous: eagles, buzzards and kestrels soared and swooped above and below us, while on one mossy pass the ladybirds were holding a love-in, hundreds of polka-dotted red bugs in a frenzy of enthusiastic reproduction, no intention of "flying away home." In a more domestic vein there were sheep by the dozens, guarded by huge and very protective dogs – no shepherds within hailing distance – and a chorus of cows that roared, bellowed and trumpeted a greeting as we trudged by.

When we were not scaling ridges exultantly, we were padding through forests so thick as to be primeval, barely fingered by the sun. Here there might be an orchid relative with mysterious tendrils or a fluorescent pink cluster of wild geraniums. But most often we seemed to be near water, balancing on stones across a rivulet, wading up or down a river, picnicking by a crystalline pool or coasting like reckless children, bumping against rocks in the mad current, over and over again. Not all of it was pleasant. A two-hour wade turned into a four-hour torment that made virtual mincemeat out of tender toes. At times we felt as though we were splashing through ice cubes, but we endured.

We were even tricked into swimming into the Apatito (Untrodden) gorge, so called because "no one" knows where it ends. The entrance is misleadingly innocent, a solarium with flat rocks for basking, but our guides fortified us with a snack of nuts and raisins and lured us into the cavern behind, barely giving us a moment to change our hiking boots for sneakers. We stepped into the shallows and were soon up to our waists in cool but not polar water. Before we knew it we were swimming into a dark chasm, where a tiny slit of blue gleamed from between luminous green cliffs that rose 10 to 15 m above us. Fig trees stuck out at right angles to these walls; nobody would ever taste their fruit. Shivering, we retraced our strokes back to the hot rocks, glad to have done it, glad it was over.

As in remote places elsewhere in Greece, you are never really alone in the Agrafa. We'd meander into a deserted hamlet to find Stavroula almost waiting for us, an audience for her stories and guests to ply with gifts of homemade cheese, bread, lettuces and spring onions. She'd given birth to her five children in her three-room house, without a doctor, of course, and now they'd gone off to Karpenissi and Athens. Maybe next winter she and her husband would join them as her former neighbours had. But habits die hard, and on another day we met a mother, muffled in black wool, with her six-year-old daughter in flipflops on their weekly three-hour "outing" to pick up mail, essentials and gossip from the nearest general store. They too belonged to a one-family village, and their jaunt in flimsy shoes would have taken us with our goretex boots double the time. We also discovered that loneliness did not mean ignorance of the outside world. An elderly history lover regaled us with the tale of Manhattan's purchase by the Dutch for $36 and a few trinkets, while a woman's wrinkles disappeared into a radiant smile as she bragged of her eight brothers thriving in New Jersey.

Of course, it is not true that history has altogether bypassed the Agrafa. Unfortunately, the region has no dearth of civil war memorials. One is particularly poignant, dedicated to the men, women and children caught in a high valley during a freak April blizzard in 1947. Communists and Republicans alike, prepared to die in battle, were discovered wrapped in each other's arms when the snow melted. But some fanatics cannot abide their reconciliation. They have defaced it every year since the monument was erected in the early 80s, leaving a tumbled pile of meaningless stones. And every year these are then painstakingly replaced and adorned with a new plaque. *(I have since learned that there are now two memorials, one for each side.)*

The Agrafa may be harsh and unforgiving – the locals are full of stories of terrible accidents from landslides, falling rocks, cars slipping over snowy roads – but to the outsider it is gracious. Poverty here breeds generosity and *philoxenia*, women who loaded our arms with spinach pies, drivers who let us clamber into their pickups. It is also beautiful beyond words. On our last day, we went to the Trypa or hole, where water showered out of the mossy riverbank and mini cataracts spilled like lace into the translucent stream. It was only 30 minutes' walk from the road and if we'd seen it earlier we could never have been induced to explore further.

Returning to Athens on the National Road, with its belching buses, rocketing lorries and desiccated verges, was tantamount to culture shock.

The Trypa gorge is only passable in summer

This article was written in 1998. Since then not much has changed except that the roads have been widened and smoothed, though they remain unasphalted. The footpaths on the other hand are, sadly, falling into disrepair. ○

How to get there

The Agrafa is most easily reached from Karpenissi in central Greece.

Call Trekking Hellas (210 3310323-6) for information about their treks, or look up www.trekking.gr or www.outdoorsgreece.com. The Agrafa walks are rated 2, of moderate difficulty.

Where to stay (area code 22370)

A few more small hotels have opened to complement *Niki's place*. If you want to make your own arrangements, here are some numbers:

Niki Komboyianni, Agrafa village (93209); *Xenonas Ta Agrafa* (93220, 6977702976) (Kostas Gatis); *Xenonas Makkas*, run by three brothers at Krendis, a great place to start or end your trip (31350).

Where else to eat

Apart from the hotels, a meal can be had at *Neromilos*, at the junction of the main road that follows the Agrafiotis river. The speciality is trout served under the plane trees. Also, look out for *Lambros's kafeneion* near the bridge before Agrafa village; his firearms hang on the wall next to the sardine cans and windex bottles.

Extra reading:
Experienced hikers wishing to explore the Agrafa on their own will find paths and routes described in *Trekking in Greece*, a *Lonely Planet* walking guide, by Marc Dubin and Michael Cullen. Tim Salmon has written a beguiling description of life among the Agrafa shepherds in *The Unwritten Places*, Lycabettus Press, Athens, 1993. And keep an eye out for a completely revised and updated edition of Tim Salmon's *The Mountains of Greece*, written in collaboration with Michael Cullen, published July, 2006, by Cicerone Press of London.

Lefkada's
local colour

Milky sands hundreds of feet below toe-curling sheer rocks, swirling azure water arranging itself in hypnotic patterns around boulders and bathers.

ts name means white (*leukos* in Greek), but it could just as easily have been named Prasinada (or Green). The northern tip is so flat it barely skims the sea, while the southern point soars dizzyingly above the waves and several peaks between them rise higher than a thousand metres. It's an island and yet you can drive there. This is Lefkada, a place full of contradictions, refusing to be pigeon-holed.

Lefkada, or more formally Lefkas, belongs to the Ionian chain, called in Greek the Eptanisa after the seven largest of them. This is another misnomer because there are at least seventeen other inhabited islands and dozens more deserted ones in the archipelago, many of them spattering the sea between Lefkada, the mainland and Ithaki and Kefalonia to the south. The proximity of their almost infinite coves and sheltered bays has made Lefkada the sailing capital of the Ionian, if not Greece – one label that actually fits.

Unless you're on a yacht, you approach Lefkada via a straight road that cuts through a lagoon. On one side an amorphous hump of grey stone – one of the area's three forts – interrupts the tangled green of the swamp; on the other, low islets ride like half-sunken barges on the glassy surface of the water, as they do on the outer reaches of the Venetian Lido. Here and there egrets peck at delicacies in the mud.

Most of the time, you cross onto the island with barely a pause to glance at the castle of Santa Maura, which guards the 20-metre-wide canal that severs Lefkada from the mainland. The first trench was dug by colonists from Corinth in the 7th century BC. The castle itself is a vestige of later conquerors – Venetians and Turks – while the saint, who gave her name to the entire island when the Venetians ruled, was a virgin martyr revered by Lefkada's first Christians. White island/black saint (*mavra* in Greek); I wonder who she was.

But sometimes, you have to wait while the floating bridge swings open to allow a procession of yachts to file through. When I first went to Lefkada in 1969, sailboats congregated at

t Agios Nikitas you get your first taste
f white Lefkada

When Onassis bought the islet of Skorpios, he laid the beaches with Saudi Arabian sand brought in his oil tankers

Nydri, halfway down the east coast. Not only was it safe and lush, it faced Skorpios, which had hit the headlines the year before when Onassis made Jackie Kennedy his wife there. Now the celebrities have vanished, Nydri has succumbed to honky-tonk tourism, and the yachts have a brand new marina at Lefkada town.

Here a forest of masts fences in the elegant post-modern buildings that house facilities, restaurants and spiffy hotels. The quay opposite hums as buses and taxis unload flotilla crews, traffic comes to a standstill, and gorgeous guys languidly flirt on cellphones from a few well-placed benches.

What had happened to the town I remembered? The drowsy, slightly shabby capital of the past seemed to have disappeared behind a wall of fastfoodadika and cafeterias crammed with frappé-sippers. To balance the smart marina, a large white theatre was being added to a new cultural centre on the northern waterfront. Were it not for a dear friend, I doubt we would have ventured behind this façade.

With F as guide, we parked at the Cultural Centre, which also contains a fine little archaeological museum, and slipped into the back streets. Immediately, we entered what may be the most unusual village in Greece. Except for Corfu and Paxi, the four main islands in the Ionian have suffered tremendously from earthquakes. The worst, in 1948 in Lefkada and 1953 in Ithaki, Kefalonia and Zakynthos, flattened some of the prettiest towns in the country. Under Venetian rule for four hundred years, their architecture reflected Italy and the Renaissance; their churches were baroque not Byzantine, and no minarets needled their skies.

The islanders faced rebuilding in various ways. The Zantiots reconstructed their town stone by stone; the army corps of engineers bulldozed Argostoli into even greater rubble and erected boring but functional houses as fast as they could. The people of Lefkada, on the other hand, thought the solution lay in making their houses light and flexible. Thus, while the ground floor may be made of conventional stone or bricks, the upper floors are wooden. But wood would never survive Lefkada's heavy rains and perennial damp, so the owners covered their walls with corrugated metal for protection. The result might have been a shanty town, but for an imaginative coat of paint.

Paying no heed to conventions governing matching and clashing, each homeowner painted his walls the shade he wanted. No house is the same; violet, orange, yellow, red, green, pink, apricot and brown may all coexist in the same block. Talk about local colour, the effect is charming.

"It's cheerful, counteracts their tendency to melancholy," said F, who grew up in Athens. "We don't have the brightness and openness of the Cyclades. On the other hand, Lefkada has more than its share of university professors, writers (like Sikelianos, Karyotakis and Valaoritis), and creative people, like Agni Baltsa, whose father was a taxi driver here."

As we plunged deeper into the back streets, F dipped into every shop like a hummingbird. She introduced us to Sideris, a watercolourist surrounded by his paintings of the island; to one of the Regantos boys, whose family run Lefkada's best known taverna; to Papadopoulos the baker, who "makes the best pastries in Greece," until we came to the main square, where her grandfather's house still stands opposite the turquoise prefectural hall.

"He was in the wine business. Lefkada's grapes are not 'grand cru' material but its wine was in great demand in France and Italy. Not for its taste but for its colour. It's such a deep red they use it for vermouth and for tinting their own paler wines. Pappou was the first to sell them the idea and export it."

As we walked down the main street, it was my turn to dive into the shops. Instead of souvenirs, they sold traditional sweets, cheeses, honey, sausages and embroideries. These last feature delicate gold thread sewn into small geometric patterns on a cream fabric, but the *pastelli* (sesame bars), nougat and almond confections proved harder to resist.

Munching on delectable and more nourishing wedges of spinach pie, we passed other examples of Lefkadan idiosyncratic architecture: bell/clock towers made of girders like a child's oversize meccano set contraption. Standing next to 17th century stone churches, they could not be more incongruous. Sadly, the churches themselves are usually locked. Although many of them survived the '48 earthquake, another strong quake in 2003 severely cracked walls and ceilings and they have yet to be repaired. But one was open, so I stepped in for a look at the elaborate iconscreen and Italianate icons that are so typically Ionian.

Inside, a little old lady was fussing with the candles. Instead of casting the malevolent eye usually thrown at a foreign woman wearing shorts, she smiled and said, "Italia"?

Half an hour later, after listening to her dissect international politics, the Greek Church and the state of the economy, peppered with hilarious observations and anecdotes, F and I reluctantly dragged ourselves away. "You'll find," said F, "that Lefkadans don't fit the mould. They're hard-working, tremendous teasers and deep thinkers."

As I thought back, I realised she was right. None of the people we had talked to in the previous three days of exploring the island had been ordinary. Take Yerasimos Filippas, who owned the hotel we stayed in at Agios Nikitas. His Ostria was the first pension in the fishing port that is now Lefkada's nicest west coast tourist enclave. He'd gone fishing himself the morning we arrived and invited us to join his feast. We'd chatted on his terrace until 2 am.

From him we learned that all Lefkada's tomato red roofs are being gradually resurfaced with pale terracotta tiles, that the villages in the interior have revived, and that we would still see women wearing the long brown skirts, grey aprons, beige chemises and black or brown tasselled shawls of earlier generations.

Porto Katsiki, voted among Greece's top ten beaches

It's at Agios Nikitas that you get your first taste of "white Lefkada". The road climbs above the town through olive groves of the Corfu variety – tall and unruly – until it suddenly bursts out above a long white beach. Beyond the village, where colonial looking pastel buildings fronted with wooden balconies still outnumber antiseismic cement constructions, the coast is a series of white beaches sliced from the base of increasingly precipitous limestone cliffs.

I had never seen these beaches before. On previous visits the road south of Agios Nikitas was prohibitively atrocious but now it is 95 percent asphalted. The only deterrent is the number of steps you have to go down and then up if you want a swim. We decided to admire them from above: milky sands hundreds of feet below toe-curling sheer rocks, swirling azure water arranging itself in hypnotic patterns around boulders and bathers. After sampling

67

bird's eye views of Kathisma, Yialos (from a leafy terrace at Athani), Egremini and Porto Katsiki, we set off for Sappho's Leap, otherwise known as Cape Doukato, at the southernmost tip of Lefkada.

How did the renowned poetess get there? Did she have to travel so far from Lesvos to find a cliff dramatic enough to throw herself over? The story goes that she was rejected by a man, that a temple of Apollo stood at the site of today's abandoned lighthouse, that young Romans used to emulate her but hedged their bets by donning feathers and having a friend with a boat wait below. Legends abound but the panoramic vista is its own reward. Ithaki and Kefalonia look close enough to swim to, the white cliffs of Meganisi a scimitar slash against the eastern horizon. We bumped back over 15 minutes of bad road, past the honey stands and fir forests and took the turn down to Vassiliki, the windsurfing mecca of the Ionian, if not all of Greece.

The place had changed enormously since we were last there fifteen years ago. Catamarans, dinghies and windsurfers were wallowing in the shallows on that windless day. Broad quays lined the waterfront, four-storey hotels climbed the hill opposite. Strangest of all was the Slavic language adorning the menus outside every taverna.

"It's Czech," explained Nasia, our young waitress. "We built too many rooms after the English started up the windsurfing schools, and now we can't fill all of them. So people started working with Czech agencies and even though the rents are minimal, the rooms are full for six months a year. The Czechs stuff their suitcases with food – tins, even spaghetti – so they don't eat out often but when they do, we're ready for them."

Was this the island's future? Tourism on the cheap. "We should have used Pelion as a model," said a woman who ran an embroidery shop in *Karyes*, the biggest mountain village. "We let people get away with doing what they wanted instead of setting standards."

Up here amidst the walnut trees, a few kilometres and an ocean of olives away from the madness of Nydri, Lefkada's beauty has barely been touched by tourism. As we drove down the mountain, a flock of bright parachutes caught our eye. Like huge butterflies, about a dozen surfers had harnessed the air to ride the waves off the Yira, the spit of sand that encircles the lagoon northwest of the town. There was nothing else along the miles of beach except four armless windmills and a taverna or two.

Lefkada wears a coat of many colours and it shouldn't be hard to find a hue that suits you.
○

How to get there

Improved roads and the new Rion-Antirrion bridge have reduced the driving time between Athens and Lefkada to less than 5 hours, if you go via Agrinio and Amfilohia after Messolonghi instead of hugging the coast. You can also fly to Aktion-Preveza, where the military airport has been expanded to handle international charters as well as domestic flights.

Island hopping

Even without a yacht, you can take a ferry from Nydri or Vassiliki to Kefalonia and Ithaki. Meganisi, with three simple villages amidst its olive groves and more white cliffs, is a short ride from Nydri, where you can also rent an outboard.

Where to stay (area code 26450)

Hotels of every description rim Lefkada's coasts and rooms can be found even in remote mountain villages. We stayed in funky *Ostria*, at the start of Agios Nikitas, which has a happy, hospitable atmosphere, a splendid view and simple rooms (97483). *Ionian Blue* (29029), between Nikiana and Nydri on the east coast, represents the other extreme: 116 luxurious rooms and suites, pools, restaurants and jacuzzis in a complex that is a marvel of environmentally sensitive design. In town we spent three pleasant nights at the Santa Maura at the north end of the main pedestrian street (21308-9).

Where to eat

For a romantic dinner at water's edge, *Koniora* at Lygia (turn off the east coast road one block south of the Shell station); for traditional Greek food at a Lefkada institution, *O Regandos*, west of the main square on Dimariou Verioti street in town (try the baked octopus) and also in town *Bibliothiki* (new in 06) for ambiance and good traditional food (follow the "library" signs); for well-cooked fish in Agios Nikitas, *Portoni* and for meat, *Lefteris*, opposite it. Among the mass of tavernas at Vassiliki, *Vagelaras* near the south end of the waterfront seems to be the most popular. Lefkada now produces very drinkable white and red wines under the label *Lefkaditiki Yi* (Lefkadan Earth).

And a word to the wise: If you want to enjoy Lefkada, do not go there in August.

From Preveza
to Igoumenitsa

Augustus wasted no time building a city to commemorate his victory, which ended the civil war that had been festering since the assassination of Uncle Julius.

(above) Kassope, ruined since Augustus emptied it to populate Nikopolis

(left) Parga's most famous landmark, viewed from its Venetian castle

This is the story of the coast of Epirus, the region rated as the poorest in the EU. I suppose those desk-bound statisticians are thinking in terms of average income or productivity, because in so many other categories Epirus can go to the top of the list. Famous for superlative mountains, stone-built villages and rivers, it is also surprisingly rich in beaches, wetlands, castles and antiquities. Finally, it has a more turbulent history than would normally be considered desirable and a reputation for breeding tough, stubborn people – most notably Pyrrhos and Ali Pasha.

This version of the story, at least, begins at the narrow strait where the huge enclosed Ambracian Gulf meets the Ionian Sea. Nowadays what is unnecessarily described as an "immersed tunnel" connects the two peninsulas, so you no longer have to board a tiny ferry at Aktion to get to Preveza.

You can slip under the narrows without giving a moment's thought to a battle fought here on a breezy afternoon in 31 BC. With some 700 ships chasing and ramming each other under a hailstorm of arrows and catapulted stones, it must have been sheer chaos. Outnumbered and outmanoeuvred by Octavian and his cunning admiral Agrippa, Cleopatra turned tail. Whether burning with love for the Egyptian queen or the treasure stowed in her galley, Antony soon followed, "like a doting mallard" (to quote Patrick Leigh Fermor). The battle of Aktion forced them to abandon their half-baked plans to invade Italy and left the way clear for Octavian to become Caesar Augustus, emperor of Rome.

Augustus wasted no time building a city to commemorate his victory, which ended the civil war that had been festering since the assassination of Uncle Julius. He also had a quick fix approach to populate his Nikopolis. His soldiers conducted a dragnet of all the towns in northwest Greece between what are now Yannina and Messolonghi. Yanked from their homes, their 200,000 inhabitants became instant Nikopolitans. But it can't have been that terrible for the city soon became a jewel in the imperial crown, the regional capital, and much more Greek than Roman. It continued to sparkle under the Byzantines after Rome fell.

Today its walls look like sleeping brick behemoths half buried under creepers and thistles. Spread over a vast area just north of Preveza, they give an idea of the size and majesty of Nikopolis but little more. Sadly, very few of these remarkable ruins are visitable.

Thirty years ago I had walked around a marvellous site, with Roman fountains, two well-preserved theatres and the shells of several early Christian basilicas with charming mosaics. But in 2005 everything was overgrown and off-lim-

Sadly, this magnificent gate leads only to overgrown ruins

its, the mosaics buried under weed-sprouting plastic sheets. A sign in front of the theatre proclaimed "Approaching is prohidited/Danger of momument parts' collapse" [sic]. The guard at the two-room museum, originally built as a storehouse, told a sad tale.

"The archaeologists had the sheds protecting the mosaics pulled down in 1984. They were hoping some benefactor would take pity on them and put up the money for new, more elegant coverings. Back then, I said I'd probably be retired by the time the new sheds were installed, and it looks like I was right. Just four more years to go."

The story got worse. The money has been raised, many times over what's needed, but now

The Nikopolis theatre is in danger of collapsing

The seasonal lake near Paramythia lies close to the Oracle of the Dead

the committee in charge can't agree on a design. A new study is submitted every year only to be rejected. Furthermore, a beautiful big museum for the Nikopolis finds was completed in 2003. It cost 2.5 billion drachma (ca 7,353,000 euros) but has yet to open. Doesn't the Archaeological Service owe the public an explanation?

Shocked and disappointed, we prowled around the stupendous walls, which have been more Byzantine than Roman since the 6th century when Justinian reinforced them to keep out the Slavs.

Preveza, on the other hand, brightened our mood. A broad esplanade along the tranquil port, carless market streets, freshly painted 19th century storefronts, a couple of Venetian-era churches (studded with marble bits and pieces from Nikopolis) – the little town wore an aura of prosperity that was certainly lacking twenty years ago. It has the quaint charm of a place that is managing quite nicely thank you without sacrificing its character to tourism. Friends tell me that it also has the best tomatoes in Greece. Sometime in mid-August Preveza holds a festival in their honour and you can walk along the waterfront, slurping up free sliced tomatoes with feta, stuffed tomatoes and other treats. Similar to American beefsteak tomatoes, they never reach Athens, so look out for them even if you miss the festival.

Though not a trace remains, Preveza has an ancient past. It was founded in the 3rd century BC by Pyrrhos who named it Berenikia after his mother-in-law. The king of Epirus may have embarked from here on his ill-fated campaigns to conquer southern Italy, Macedonia and the Peloponnese. A cousin of the Great Alexander, Pyrrhos possessed the same insatiable thirst for battle but never knew when to stop. Although he created a Greater Epirus, founded many cities and built the theatre at Dodoni, we only remember his name as a metaphor for disastrous victories.

Berenikia was swallowed up by Nikopolis and resurfaced as Preveza around the 12th century. From then until 1912, the port on the strait changed hands like a hot potato, as the usual suspects – Normans, Venetians, Ottomans, Barbarossa, Ali Pasha and even Napoleon – vied for control, erecting three castles and repeatedly razing homes in the process. From 1881 to 1912 an imaginary line through the strait marked the border between free Greece and the Ottoman Empire.

Just north of Preveza in the Zalongo mountains there are two must-see sites that bridge the region's bloody history. Deserted since Augustus's conquest, ancient Kassope overlooks lagoon and sea from a plateau surrounded by steep grey cliffs flecked with green. High above the neat rectangles marking city walls and houses, a line of stark white female figures, tall as cypresses, marches to its death, hand in hand.

Every Greek schoolchild knows the legend of the women of Souli, who in 1803 rather than face capture by Ali Pasha's soldiers, threw their sons and daughters over the cliff and then, dancing and singing, leapt after them. The Souliots were like the Cretans, a thorn in the side of the Turks, constantly rebelling against Ottoman rule. When Ali Pasha became governor of Epirus in 1789, he vowed to crush the whole clan. Fourteen years later, they were still uncowed, so he besieged their villages and coaxed them out with promises of a truce. Trickery succeeded where force had failed but when the Souliots realised he meant to hold them captive, many managed to escape over the mountains to Agrafa. The sixty who remained, including a few men, eluded him in a more drastic way.

I'm afraid I was too much of a wimp to climb the 300 steps up to the monument in the noonday sun. I persuaded myself that the colossal cement statues, a work of George Zongolopoulos before his fascination with umbrellas, were poignant and dramatic enough from below. And they did send goosebumps prickling down our arms despite the heat.

Kassope predates the Souliot tragedy by almost two thousand years. It must have been a pleasant place to live, with a wonderful view, a comfortable inn with individual hearths in the guestrooms, a bustling agora, paved roads with drainage channels and two theatres. It would have been civilised and fairly peaceful until the Romans destroyed it, not once but twice in the space of a century and a half. I thought of the women having to leave their airy mountain homes for humid, mosquito-plagued Nikopolis. At least they were given new ones.

If you continue over Zalongo, which is an anthill compared to the peaks of the Pindos further north, following signs for Paramythia and Kanalaki to Mesopotamos, the road will eventually bring you to the Oracle of the Dead. The grey stone buildings sit on the north bank of the Acheron river, up which Charon used to ferry the dead to Hades. The ancients believed that the spot where the river disappeared underground was one of the four entrances to Pluto's kingdom.

Contrary to expectation, the Nekromanteion conjured neither spooky visions nor sad memories. But maybe that's because we had not prepared for this early version of the séance. In the old days, anxious for news of deceased loved ones, we would have spent a month (and who knows how many drachmas?) purifying ourselves at the sanctuary. The priests would have plied us with lupin seeds and raw broad beans, the ancient equivalent of peyote, until we were open to any suggestion. Then, they would have ushered us down a hole into a tunnel-like crypt with fifteen arches. There we would communicate with the shades of the dead, provided we never revealed what we had seen and heard. One whisper and the gods of the Underworld would wreak their revenge.

Those priests were masters in the arts of deception and illusion. Dressed in black, they concealed themselves in the crevices between the crypt's thick arches and in secret corridors that muffled their voices. They even manipulated an elaborate winch in order to dangle ghostlike figures before the droopy eyes of the credulous pilgrims. What else would you expect from the society that invented theatre?

Although some of the walls look Cyclopean, the Oracle opened in the 7th century BC and

**In this murky crypt pilgrims hoped
to communicate with the spirits of loved ones**

the ruins are actually Hellenistic. Rustic polygonal masonry must have been in fashion then because Kassope is full of it, too. Square rooms arranged around a courtyard, the sanctuary greatly resembles a monastery, an impression strengthened by the incongruous presence of an 18th century chapel. The Romans, yes, them again, burned the sanctuary in 167 BC.

From here you can forget about antiquity and steep yourself in nature. Upstream at Glyki are the Acheron springs, where plane tree forests, cold green water and café/restaurants meet. If your ankles can bear it, you can wade up the gorge, but there are also drier paths (one up to the deserted Souliot strongholds) and the possibility of rafting. Downstream on the coast at Ammoudia, the Acheron delta offers glimpses of exotic marsh birds and a long stretch of sand. I wished we'd had the time to take the boat ride up the river to the Oracle (and, of course, back); never mind that the last 2 km are on foot.

From Ammoudia, it's a short drive to Parga. The road climbs above tantalising coves, variations on the unbeatable theme of turquoise sea, emerald shores and ivory beach. In such a setting, Parga should be a dream come true. But in the words of some well-travelled Dutch grecophiles we encountered, "It has sold out to tourism, the tavernas try to gyp you, and you never hear a word of Greek."

We walked up the back streets to the Norman/Venetian castle, where the old barracks have been restored into a peaceful café. Just before the gate, I stepped into a restaurant to look at the view. As I stood on the balcony, the owner said, "See that castle across the way? The Turks used to shoot their cannons at us from there. They tried for years to conquer us, but their cannonballs always fell short. After the Second World War, when my father was a boy, he used to dive for them in the bay and sell them to help feed the family. He kept two. I've put them on this railing as decoration.

Splendid walks start from the Acheron springs, both in and out of the water

"But Ali Pasha got what he wanted without a fight. When the British took over the Ionian islands and Parga, they sold Parga to him. The Greeks here were so disgusted and horrified they fled to Corfu, taking their ancestors' bones with them. They did not come back until 1913, when Epirus was finally free."

This was not the only time I heard this story. What struck me was that everyone told it as if it had happened yesterday instead of almost two hundred years ago. Memories have a long shelf life in this part of the world.

For a taste of Epirus without them, you can beach hop all the rest of the way to Igoumenitsa. There are dozens of dream coves around Syvota and Arillas where all this history will melt into an advertisement for summer in Greece: sun, sea, sand and you know what. ○

Where to stay

Enetico, on the outskirts of Parga, is a good base for exploring and also has a pool and an Italian chef (26840 32900). Otherwise, you can find everything from fancy resort hotels to simple rooms and campings in Parga and in Syvota and elsewhere on the coast.

Where to eat

Look for *The Deck* at the Parga marina; it was brand new in 2005. *The Castello* (Italian) restaurant a couple of blocks inland comes highly recommended. Don't miss the café up in the Castle for a snack or drink with a splendid view. At the Acheron springs there are several restaurants and tavernas; some advertise trout.

A funerary statue from the area of the ancient theatre of Nikopolis

A day in Paxi:
small is beautiful

I like to think of Poseidon
as a master jeweller,
carving each beach into
a bagatelle for his beloved
and then placing it in
a setting of water the colour
of jade, celadon, emerald,
sapphire, turquoise,
aquamarine or lapis lazuli.

We are guidebook writers on a mission: to "do" Paxi in a day. My friend the Fish and I have got a tight schedule, an even tighter budget, so what are we doing draping ourselves in dozens of pareus in a boutique in Lakkos when we should be checking out its bars and restaurants? But the proprietors are so welcoming, their Balinese prints so beguiling, we can find no compelling reason to tear ourselves away. Since arriving on the island with the early morning hydrofoil from Corfu, we have succumbed to a delicious lack of urgency, a feeling that life has slowed down

Wooded islets and a fjordlike inlet
shield Gaios from the open sea

Other than fish from its fishermen, and olives from its olive groves, everything on Paxi is imported

to a languorous crawl and that the pleasure principle is the only one that really matters.

Somewhere else time may be important but not here. After all, you could drive round Paxi in half an hour, it's only 9.5 km long, 3 km wide, a mere speck in the ocean. The ancients said that Poseidon created it by striking Corfu with his trident. He wanted a bower where he could woo his amour of the moment, the nymph Amphitrite. So he speared off a chunk of the bigger island which shattered into Paxi, Antipaxi

and a few even tinier islets and lost his trident in the process. In another era, the Paxians found it and adopted it as their symbol. This splintering into several islands also explains why Paxi is usually referred to in the plural ("oi" in Greek instead of the singular "os").

I discovered the myth this morning in a guidebook I picked up in the National Bank branch in the main port Gaios, named after the disciple of St. Paul who brought Christianity to the island. The bank is actually nothing more than a cashier's guichet in an old-fashioned hardware store/ships chandlers with ropes and buoys hanging from the rafters, multi-litre paint cans pyramided against the walls. Spyros Bogdanos sat comfortably at the till with copies of his book, *Paxoi from Yesterday to Today,* displayed behind him, obviously feeling no qualms about wearing his hats as bank manager and author at the same time (and currently mayor of the island, too). And when I explained my purpose here, he even volunteered to open the museum this afternoon before the hydrofoil departs for Corfu.

Further down the back street, which seems to have no name, some of the old stone houses have been done up as modest stores. Most have beach towels and sundresses dangling outside them, but one is a gallery exhibiting startling silver eyes embedded in dazzling white

The main port of Gaios, named after a disciple of St Paul

stones to keep bad luck at bay. Rounding a corner returned me to the waterfront where fishermen were unloading their catch of groupers and dogfish. Another kaiki had brought crates of bananas, tomatoes and kiwis, sacks of aubergines and potatoes, plaits of onions and garlic. Paxi has to import everything it needs, except olives and olive oil, from Corfu and Igoumenitsa. Even water.

There were yachts and dinghies parked along the quay, travel bureaus in many of the pale ochre neoclassical buildings opposite. I dipped in and out of them, asking questions in some, filching brochures from others where the staff were evidently out for a coffee. In the Agricultural Bank the queue was moving slowly even though customers and tellers exchanged greetings and gossip with the rapidity of jackhammers, rounded syllables cascading off their tongues as if they were performing in a Rossini opera. Passing one darkened doorway, I caught a pungent whiff of olive oil and regretted not having a canister. Paxi oil is renowned for its sweetness and purity, and this warehouse (no name, no sign) from the past is one place where you can buy it. Nearby rises the island's tallest building, Governor's House, where during the 18th and 19th centuries the representatives of first the Doge of Venice and then the Queen of England resided until 1864, when Paxi and the rest of the Ionian islands were finally united with Greece. The ground floor of the mansion has received a new coat of yellow paint, but the three upper stories are still a faded, charmingly dappled peach, ivory and grey. The museum is in here so I'd be back.

Historically, Paxi usually shared the fate of Corfu. A few important naval battles were fought nearby in antiquity – Syvota, Aktion; it had its share of Latin conquerors and murderous raids by pirates and Turks. But being so small and poor, it was never the main prize and there are few monuments demanding one's pilgrimage. The absence of sights with a capital "S" was very soothing to this harried fact collector.

I wandered back to the square where the Fish was sitting with local friends, Mary and Malcolm. They were catching up on the latest news in one of its eight cafés with the doctor, the lawyer, the builder, the mayor and a handful of other ex-pats who just happened to pass by. The excursion boats hadn't arrived yet, so

Paxi's population was still at its normal 2,300 people. There was also a pleasant air of relaxed activity, which they said inevitably turns into a rush hour scramble around noon when the day trippers pour in by the hundreds. Mary drew my attention to the far end of the waterfront where a statue painted a virulent shade of green stood uncertainly in a shorn-off bronze rowboat. "See that guy? He's a Revolutionary hero who single-handedly tried to torch the Turkish fleet. Some irreverent souls call him the 'Unknown Tourist'."

We clambered into Malcolm's vintage Jeep and rattled out of town, stopping above Gaios for a classic photo of the fjord-like entrance to the port. From the sea you can't even spot Gaios, concealed as it is behind a couple of wooded islets, one sporting the ruined Venetian castle of Agios Nikolaos, the other the Panayia church, the scene of feasting and dancing on August 15th. The water curves round them like a river, leaving any bad weather out at sea.

But there was no hint of bad weather on this hot June morning and the huge dam/cistern built with EU money outside of town to catch the winter rains lay empty but for a puddle of sodden leaves and bloated frogs. Millions were given for this ugly ill-conceived pond lined with black rubber, instead of on the more obvious, practical solution of a regular water-boat serv-

Voutoumi beach on Antipaxi is Poseidon's masterpiece

ice. Still, this is Paxi's only eyesore, for the island is one big olive grove, with pitted, gnarled, sinewy olive trees, and walls made of square, lichen-speckled white stones. As in Corfu, the trees are a Venetian legacy; not only did they offer a bonus for every 100 planted, they also showed the Paxians how to build the walls and terraces that support them. In some areas the branches hanging over the road have been lopped off. "Talk about oil slick," said Malcolm, who fell in love with Paxi twenty years ago.

"Squashed olives can make the road so slippery they cause accidents, so the trees have to be trimmed."

We passed a signpost showing risible distances – "2 km Longos, 5 km Lakkos," dropped Mary and Malcolm off at their home and lurched off in the Jeep to explore. For the rest of the morning they would receive phone calls to the tune of: "Why didn't you stop by when you were in the neighbourhood?" and "Did you know that some people have got your car?

They stopped for petrol a little while ago." Paxi is that sort of island, possessive and protective; not a place where you can keep a secret long.

Driving around "on the roads marked in red on the map so you don't hit a dead end," I wanted to take some more photos but it's hard to get an angle on Paxi. The walls and olive groves, so attractive and restful to the eye, are cloaked in shadow; the grizzled four-house hamlets, the baroque Venetian belfries, even the ruined olive presses with their great stone wheels standing upright amidst the rusted machinery don't seem to fit into the camera lens with enough contrast or depth. But if the interior of the island is blissfully unphotogenic, the vistas on the coasts can keep you snapping for hours.

I like to think of Poseidon as a master jeweller, carving each beach into a bagatelle for his beloved and then placing it in a setting of water the colour of jade, celadon, emerald, sapphire, turquoise, aquamarine or lapis lazuli. He made the eastern coves gentle and romantic, with flat white rocks or smooth white pebbles and sand, fringed with trees almost to the water's edge. Perfect for seduction. But when he styled the west coast, he clearly wanted to impress, awe, perhaps even frighten her. Here are stark white cliffs soaring out of the sea, caves, rock bridges, castles and cathedrals. I cannot think of anywhere else where so much beauty is packed into such a small place. And this of course is what the day trippers come to see. This shore and Voutoumi beach on Antipaxi, which is Poseidon's masterpiece. It's been voted one of the most beautiful beaches in the Mediterranean, and it is mesmerising. If Amphitrite didn't fall for the god when he presented her with Voutoumi, then she would not have been worth wooing.

Back in Longos, a tiny horseshoe-shaped port which prides itself on being the only village in Greece without a single plastic chair, we try to choose a taverna for lunch with Mary and Malcolm. It's not easy, not only because all six are excellent, but because they don't want to be seen as playing favourites. Corfiots descend here just to dine at Katharantzos or Vassilis, but we've got to catch a boat and opt for quick and friendly O Yios. Besides, Vassilis' customers have to be prepared to leap up from their seats when the bus rolls through – that's how wee the port is.

Over a little wine, whitebait and courgette fritters, we fall into a benign state of inertia and somehow forget the appointment with Mr Bogdanos at the museum. In photos it looks charming and interesting, filled with memorabilia ranging from prehistoric pots to 19th century Victoriana. But it will have to wait until next time. Paxi may be small but it's neither possible nor wise to do it in one day. My apologies, I'm afraid I succumbed to letting Paxi "do" me. ○

How to get there

Paxi can be reached by ferry, hydrofoil and excursion boat from Corfu, Igoumenitsa and Parga. More exciting, in 2004 AirSea Lines inaugurated hydroplane flights between Corfu and Paxi, which take only 15 minutes, though they also offer a longer, "sightseeing route" when enough passengers are interested. For more information, check out www.airsealines.com

The best way to get to know the island is to walk, but by all means rent a boat with an outboard motor and explore the west coast and Antipaxi at your own speed. Paxi and Antipaxi (which has only 20 inhabitants) have been favourites with yachting jet-setters since the 60s when the paparazzi discovered it while chasing Onassis and Jacqueline.

Venetian belfries are the norm in Paxi

Where to stay

In the high season accommodation is very restricted, but Christos Grammatikos at Paxos Magic Holidays (26620 32440, fax 32122), info@paxosmagic.gr) or Anna Aperghi in Corfu (26610 48713/14, fax 48715, aperghi@travelling.gr) may be able to help. In spring or fall prospects are better. A friend recommends *Pithari Villas*, owned by Villy Malami, in Gaios (26620 32491).

Where to eat

In Gaios, at *Taka Taka*, an elegant taverna/bar set in a lovely garden, where grilled goodies including suckling pig rule the menu. Dinner only; open from early spring to mid-autumn. Or *Mambo*, right on the waterfront, run by a bevy of gorgeous women, who serve oversized portions of delectable traditional Greek dishes.

And in Lakka, *La Bocca*, the domain of a Torino-born, Paris-trained, Buddhist chef who does amazing things with salads and seafood. Wonderful view, at the far right of the waterfront.

Paradise lost?
Corfu revisited

Corfu is still Greece's Garden Isle par excellence. And its all-pervasive greenness is awesome to one accustomed to the sere, treeless Aegean. Most of it is so lush that a multitude of sins are hidden or at least muted under a mantle of vines and trees.

W hen I told a friend I'd just come back from Corfu, her nose wrinkled in disgust. "They've ruined it," she sneered. "The last time we were in Palaiokastritsa, we couldn't even swim the water was so dirty, Sidari's famous Canal d'Amour was lined with beach umbrellas and Roda looked like a poor imitation of an Athens suburb."

She was right, of course. Some parts of Corfu are so blighted you want to cry. A telecommunications spire, painted red and white and modelled on the Eiffel Tower, jabs the sky from within the courtyard of the 14th century monastery on Mount Pantokrator. Agios Stephanos on the northwest coast, windswept and empty the last time I saw it in 1990, is now home to dozens of small cheaply-built hotels catering exclusively to packaged Brits or Germans. Benitses, the island's most famous tourist slum, is trying to improve its image but is having trouble finding tenants for its domitory-like rooming houses with their paper-thin walls. Thankfully, the lager louts have since been quarantined down south at Kavos, along with others whose idea of a holiday is Sex Foam parties, Bargain Booze, fast food and karaoke, pool halls with cinema seats for viewing football matches, Bungee Rockets ("come to s_ _t yourself") and not a single Greek word to be seen, even in transliteration.

We were so depressed after crawling through endless kilometres of that creepy place (is this really what the modern world is coming

If you look beyond the tourists, the old town will draw you into its narrow streets

to?) that we drove off towards the salt flats where there's not a sign of human life. Apart from a ruined Venetian warehouse there are no buildings either, nothing but tall grasses, reeds, and birds, poking long beaks into the mud, skittering along the shore, sending ripples through the calm water. The curlew, sandpipers and plovers paid us no heed, the egrets stood aloof in the distance, but the red-legged, black-winged stilts were furious at our intrusion into their territory. They squawked and shrieked, whirled and dived while we gaped, as though turned to stone.

On the way back to town, after Messongi we swivelled up the west coast via the thinnest road on the map. The olive groves are so dense that driving through them is like entering a tunnel. There's a constant play of light and shadow, of sunglasses removed and stuck back on. These are trees out of story books, with eyes, mouths and scraggly arms; trees that might speak to you or grab you if you ventured here alone at dusk. The black nets stretched beneath them to make olive collection easier add to the spookiness. But higher up the mountain, through gaps in the foliage, the hillsides are simply gloriously green, quilted with olive trees as soft as moss, cypress trees poking through like exclamation points and here and there a patch of beige, ochre or cream made by the roofs of a distant village.

Up close the villages are not always quite as "picturesque" as promised. Aluminium doors and windows may scar old pastel façades, but the villagers' "green fingers" have worked miraculous cover-ups. Bougainvilleas in every shade of red burst up and down walls, pink ivy-leaved geraniums tumble over balconies, lavender and white African daisies cascade along with them. Snapdragons and capers billow unbidden from roof tiles or a crack in the plaster. But perhaps the most ubiquitous flower this year is the red and yellow striped lily, amaryllis, whether in pots, feta tins or in the earth. There's hardly a house without several, though in Athens you hardly ever see one.

After all Corfu is still Greece's Garden Isle par excellence. And its all-pervasive greenness is awesome to one accustomed to the sere, treeless Aegean. Most of it is so lush that a multitude of sins are hidden or at least muted under a mantle of vines and trees. This is especially true of the east coast north of the town. Though the main road as far as Ipsos passes through a dreary strip of tacky tourist enclaves, the olive trees take over just a few blocks to the left and right. Yes, Kontokali, Gouvia and Dassia do have large districts claimed by monstrous resort hotels but their grounds are surprisingly attractive and quiet, while the lanes veering inland meander to aristocrats' villas and peasant cottages sleeping through the coastal hullabaloo.

The area between Pyrgi and Kassiopi is also villa land, but these are monopolised by three British firms. Even Corfiot agents have to rent through them, leaving us peons to scramble for a handful of assorted rooms. Here there has been some "inappropriate" building – the puce monstrosity at Kalami is a glaring affront to the otherwise respectable cove where Lawrence Durrell wrote *Prospero's Cell* – but it diminishes the further north you go. And the views still coax gasps of admiration from the most grudging pessimists.

Some minutes past Kassiopi lies another well-kept secret antidote to development blues. At Agios Spyridon, an unspoilt beach, there is also a lagoon-like lake with an ominous name. Antiniotissa trips nicely on the tongue but it means "anti youth" and in past centuries scores of young people died of malaria borne by the mosquitos that thrived here. Nowadays birds flock to its still waters rather than pestilential insects, and a sheep path leads to an abandoned monastery and lonely beaches where sea lilies grow. So far no one has thought of setting up a pizzeria or a stand selling inflatable alligators and ET dolls.

Directly opposite, a few kilometres up Mt. Pantokrator, Ano Peritheia is a whole abandoned village that has only just begun to attract notice. Founded in Byzantine times as a refuge

from both pirates and malaria, its occupants moved down to the coast after World War II when DDT eradicated the bugs. Now a wonderful taverna has opened to feed trekkers, and the only salesman is a curious figure named Paul who will try to persuade you to buy his plaster casts of kittens and the goddess Athena!

For the moment Ano Peritheia has no "Sunset" bars, hotels or tavernas. Sunset-watching has inspired a cottage industry in Corfu, which may be even more flourishing than Santorini's. Kaiser Wilhelm I was perhaps the first to start the trend and even had a little "throne" erected at Pelekas from where he could gaze over most of the island. In fact, anywhere along Corfu's majestic western shores can lay claim to being the "best" vantage point.

Evening is certainly the best time to visit Palaiokastritsa, after 6 or 7 when the tour buses have wheezed back to the resorts, for the place

Palaiokastritsa's famous peacock-coloured bays seem even more gorgeous from above

the castle itself, where you can see all the way to the twin peaks of the Old Fort in Corfu Town. In 2000 the castle door was barred and a large sign with the EU logo proclaimed the allocation of billions of drachmas for its "anadeixi and axiopoiisi", dire words that translate as "to enhance and upgrade" but which usually mean to gentrify and commercialise. A souvenir stand and caretaker's booth are nearing completion and the steps up are being widened and smoothed. Can this 12th century ruin which held out against pirate and Turkish raids survive 21st century good intentions?

We broke off our reveries and drove off to the Palaiokastritsa monastery, probably the most heavily trafficked site in all Corfu with the possible exception of the Achilleion. Hordes of people are herded through it every day and the monks are reputedly fed up with the whole routine. When we arrived, the monastery was empty except for the caretakers watering sweet-smelling potted plants under the broad arches. Because I have always gone at midday I never suspected serenity lurked within its walls. I

is like a ravaged movie queen who should not be glimpsed in a noonday glare. The unparalelled beauty of turquoise and green, sea and cliffs, cannot be denied but the welter of hotels, restaurants and bars have done their damage and it's more stunning viewed from afar. Though most tourists are taken to Bella Vista at Lakones to feast their eyes, I like the view from Krini above Angelokastro better, either from the Sunset taverna's veranda or from the ramparts of

Begun in the 10th century
by the Byzantines, the Old Fort
continues to dominate
the town's skyline

had never even noticed how lovely the church is, with its uncharacteristically simple icon screen – uncarved white marble painted with blue fronds and rosettes and trimmed with gold – and superb 17th century icons, described to us with remarkable patience by the attendant. The gardens drew me outside again and over to the railing. I peered down and saw a wondrous sight – a series of coves without a single building.

Back at the entrance we heard a disconcerting cry and looked around to find a peacock flaring its tail, a perfect mirror of all the colours in the sea below.

No, I don't think Corfu is ruined. So much of it is magical, especially if you stay away from the tawdry resorts. Never mind if your guidebook says that there are 35 wonderful churches in Ano Korakiana and you can't get into any of them because the priest in Kato Korakiana is the only one with the key. There will be wild delphiniums, gladioli, and orchids at your feet, swallows swooping through the air, a Venetian belfry vying with the cypresses, and a gentle man named Spyros to point the way if you get lost.

The Liston arcades, designed by the same architect as the rue de Rivoli in Paris

This article was written in 2000. Since then, a number of changes have occurred. Benitses has reinvented itself as an attractive place to dine and boasts a new 96-berth marina; the Venetian salt warehouses have been restored though plans to turn them into a cultural centre have not yet materialised; Ano Peritheia is becoming a tad twee, with the addition of three more tavernas and two tourist shops; Angelokastro seems to be shut; and Antiniotissa can be included in the refrain of "development blues". An 800-bed resort complex has opened there and two more are going up. But The Corfu Trail, stretching the length of the island, is open. Walking all or part of it would guarantee your immersion into unspoilt Corfu.

On a more ominous note, we have the threat to Corfu's unique olive trees posed by the iniquitous deal made between a certain Corfiot supermarket and some Italians. In the past few years, some eight percent of the trees have been cut, sawn into logs and shipped across the Adriatic to stoke Italian pizza ovens. The trucks return loaded with cheap pasta, tuna and other products for distribution around the island. In September 2005, Nikos Georgiadis, MP for Corfu, introduced legislation that seeks to impose stiffer penalties for cutting these magnificent, irreplaceable trees. ⭘

How to get there
By plane or by ferry from Patras or Igoumenitsa.

Where to stay (area code 26610)
In town, I stay at the B´ class *Bella Venezia* (open all year (44290, 46500, belvenht@hol.gr) and wish I could afford the more upmarket *Cavalieri* (39336, info@cavalieri-hotel.com March-October). The *Pelecas Country Club* (52239, reservations@country-club.gr Jan-Oct) is elegant, comfortable and pricy, while *Casa Lucia's* laid-back cottages on the road to Palaiokastritsa offer New Age activities like yoga, tai chi and reiki (91419, caslucia@otenet.gr April-Oct).

Where to eat
My favourites: for Italian cooking in town *La Famiglia*, Kandouni Bizi (30270) or *La Cucina*, Guilford and Giallina streets (45029); for lunch in town on the Liston, the *Rex*; for huge portions of sizzling meat, *The Five Sisters*, near the port at 151 Stratigou St. (38263); for incredible prawn pilaf with garlic, hot peppers and garlic plus a host of other remarkable dishes, *Toula's* (26630 91350) on the water at Agni on the northeast coast; and for wonderful fish and seafood, including tiny, spicy fried lake shrimp and baby kalamarakia, *Spiros Karidis* at Boukari, south of Messongi (26620 51205).

Tip: There are also three delightful books to help you regain paradise in Corfu: *The Second Book of Corfu Walks* by Hilary Whitton Paipeti (Hermes Press and Production, Corfu, 1999, now out of print), *In the Footsteps of Lawrence Durrell and Gerald Durrell in Corfu*, also by Hilary Whitton Paipeti (Hermes Press and Production, 1998) and *Landscapes of Corfu* by Noel Rochford (Sunflower Books, London, 1999).

PART TWO

Epirus and northern Macedonia

Yannina, city on the lake

During Ali's long governorship, the bloody heads of his latest victims decorated the gateposts, while inside the palace he entertained distinguished foreigners like Lord Byron, European diplomats and merchants, favourite generals and future Greek revolutionaries.

Ali Pasha, the Lion of Yannina

The first thing you notice about the capital of Epirus (*Ipeiros*) is that it does not look Greek. The old city of Yannina (officially Ioannina) juts into a large green lake surrounded by even greener trees. Needle-sharp minarets and slate-domed mosques break through the foliage; snow-capped mountains embrace the lake, which sends back their reflection. It could be Geneva on the Bosphoros.

If you think that Yannina was Turkish for almost five hundred years and that the male population wore fezzes until 1913, this Anatolian heritage is not surprising. Even so, when freedom came elsewhere in Greece, minarets were toppled as the symbol of the oppressor. Except for those in Thrace, which still supports a Muslim minority, I can remember seeing only one or two others intact on the mainland.

Strangely, too, for such a beautifully situated town, Yannina has no ancient predecessors. Medieval texts mention a community named after a monastery dedicated to St. John (Ioannis/Yannis) the Baptist in the 9th and 10th centuries, but its history doesn't really begin until

slan Pasha's 17th century mosque,
ne of Greece's finest Islamic monuments

Ali Pasha's treasury, now filled with Yannina's famed silverware

after 1204. The nefarious conquest of Constantinople engineered by the Doge of Venice sent refugees scurrying westward. Some of them ended their flight on the island in Lake Pamvotis; others did not rest until they reached Corfu.

Accounts of the next few centuries read like a chaotic round robin, with Greeks establishing the Despotate of Epirus as an alternate Byzantine kingdom while Serbian, Albanian and Italian nobility hotly disputed their claims. Outright feuding came to a close in 1440 when the Ottoman Turks assumed control, only to flare up again in the 20th century.

As we drove into town on a busy weekend in June, Yannina looked as though it was still under siege. Friends had warned that roadworks might make it impossible to reach the lakefront, while my ten-year-old *Blue Guide* advised ominously, "Motorists should note that the one-way system is impenetrable."

Despite their predictions, we breezed through the gates of the castle right to our hotel without getting lost once. Although Yannina has long since outgrown its walls, the atmosphere within them is decidedly old world. Outside the castle, the city is prey to the traffic snarls, anonymous apartment and office blocks, and exaggerated decibels that reign in most Greek metropolises. Step inside and the lanes are miraculously quiet, the houses rarely higher than two floors and painted mellow shades of peach, apricot, pink, blue and cream. Miraculously, they are neither cute nor kitsch.

Besides houses, the castle encloses all sorts of more imposing relics of its glory time, when Yannina was a centre of culture and trade rivalled only by Salonica. Most of these lie within two citadels, slightly elevated above the rest of the city and surrounded by their own fortifications.

The larger of the two, Its Kaleh, still bears the stamp of Ali Pasha.

The legendary maverick erected the walls, the severe stone mosque and the cookhouse (now a café), topped with five chimneys that are remarkably similar to chefs' hats. But the tranquil space conveys nothing of either the splendour or

Ali Pasha's private mosque inside Its Kaleh, where Ali also had his palace

cruelty of the tyrant's seraglio. During Ali's long governorship (1788-1822), the bloody heads of his latest victims decorated the gateposts, while inside the palace he entertained distinguished foreigners like Lord Byron, European diplomats and merchants, favourite generals and future Greek revolutionaries. He welcomed them with every excess expected of an Oriental potentate:

nightingales, flaxen-haired boys, eunuchs, over-stuffed pillows, hubble-bubbles and tremendous charm and intelligence. His merry blue eyes belied his murderous reputation.

Ali was born in Tepeleni, Albania, and though he lost his father fairly early, he possessed that valuable asset – an ambitious mother, who encouraged his career moves. By virtue of what Osbert Lancaster calls "a skilful mixture of intrigue, fraud and homicide [he managed] to secure the pashalik" or governorship of Epirus before he was forty. Using the same methods, he extended his rule as far east as Evia and south to the gulf of Corinth. But by suppressing revolt within his realm, he created superb conditions for Yannina's merchants, whose caravans loaded with silverware, leather, furs and silks travelled all over the Balkans, Russia and western Europe. Naturally, he got his percentage of their earnings, which he shared less and less with his overlord, the Sultan.

Ali's nasty streak was sometimes kept in check by his favourite wife, a Greek named Kyra Vassiliki, whom he'd loved from when she was twelve. By pleading for her countrymen, she saved many of their heads from rolling. Even she could not prevent one of Ali's most horrifying acts. It took him two days to make up his mind, but finally he ordered the drowning of seventeen "women of easy virtue" together with a noble Greek woman, Kyra Frossyni – because his son's wife accused her of adultery or possibly because she wouldn't share his own bed. Sometimes the Lion of Yannina reminds me of the former Butcher of Baghdad.

In the end, Ali Pasha's appetite for power and independence proved too much for the Sublime Porte. In 1820, the Sultan dispatched an army to bring him into line. Holed up in the Castle, Ali resisted a two-year siege, but met his end when he sought refuge in a monastery on the island in the lake with Kyra Vassiliki. Fittingly, Ali's own head was sent to decorate the gates of Constantinople; Vassiliki was merely exiled there. His body was buried next to the mosque, covered with an elaborate wrought-iron cage that looks like a rococo aviary. His palace burned to the ground in 1870.

The Byzantine Museum that has taken its place presents a far different image. Traditional chants set the mood for viewing photos, icons, sculpture and ceramics from the basilicas of Nikopolis, Arta and smaller towns, as well as Yannina up to the 19th century. The exhibition continues in a small building to the right of the main entrance. Just one room, this used to be Ali Pasha's treasury. Now it is filled with some of the wonderful silver – belts, boxes, jewellery – for which Yannina's artisans are famous.

As we wandered round the Kastro by day

Typical sights within the castle walls

and by night we kept stumbling across vestiges of the Ottoman era. An enormous 50-windowed building turned out to have housed Ali Pasha's riding school. A weed-tufted dome belonged to an abandoned hammam. A simple stone façade with a star of David over the locked door was the only reminder of Yannina's once substantial Jewish community. In March 1944, virtually all of the city's two thousand Greek-speaking Romaniote Jews, whose roots in Greece date back to Augustus if not Alexander the Great, were deported to Auschwitz. A mere fifty live in Yannina now.

In the Kastro's other citadel a mosque built in the 17th century by Aslan Pasha is a tribute to Yannina's former multi-culti mix. As the Municipal Museum, it exhibits Greek costumes, weapons and jewellery; Ottoman silks, brass objects and furniture; and Jewish documents, more costumes and synagogue screens. But the mosque itself is a work of art inside and out. A slate roof spreads like an apron under the dome and minaret and over white plaster walls broken up by almost continuous tall windows.

Inside, delicate geometrical patterns in red, grey and black frame the high white dome and corners, producing an almost ethereal lightness. Together with the Imaret in Kavala, it is one of Greece's finest Islamic monuments.

It was evening when we emerged outside the castle walls. Walking along them in the direction of the lake, we passed one silver shop after another. At first I lingered – what female can resist the lure of a new pair of earrings or a bracelet? Some trinkets, though made yesterday, were almost as enticing as the pieces in the museum. My spouse's glazed look of infinite resignation tore me loose.

As we got closer to the lake, the noise engulfed us. Coming from a row of trendy cafés, the babble of Yannina's jeunesse dorée combined with the music of a dozen different sound systems sent my hands to my ears. Each establishment looked so ineffably chic – white awnings, plump sofas, elegant wooden tables – they could have illustrated *Architectural Digest*, but I knew that breakfast would be the only time I could have enjoyed sitting there.

We pushed through them towards the quieter restaurant zone, where each taverna window had five or six spits whirling with meaty temptations. In Yannina, the souk mentality prevails. Professions stick together here, as they do from Cairo to Marrakesh. And craving Eastern

food, we sat down at *Stin Ithaki*. Contrary to its name, its menu is Turkish not Ionian.

Protected by the awning from a gentle drizzle, we watched the lights switch on round the lake, twinkling constellations that revealed the existence of other gathering spots under the thick trees between the castle walls and the calm lake. Rowers in single and double sculls glided over the surface like Jurassic water beetles until the drizzle became a downpour.

The next day, dry and sunny, we did what every tourist does in Yannina: we hopped on a boat to the reedy shores of the island, generically referred to as Nisi. Everyone comes here for the thrill of seeing the monastic cell where Ali Pasha met his comeuppance, so we obediently followed the signs. But a few years ago a tree fell on Agios Panteleimon monastery, the floor with the bullet holes has been replaced, and the little museum does not do justice to the legend. We should have saved our energy for the real prize – the two main monasteries (of the seven) founded by refugee Byzantine families in the 13th century.

Both the Philanthropinos and Stratigopoulos (or Dilios) monasteries are dedicated to St. Nicholas. Both are guarded by formidable old crones who will unlock the doors in exchange for a tip, while complaining about their lumbago and eyeing you suspiciously as you examine the

One of many such monastery cloisters on the island

extraordinary frescoes that cover every square inch of the church walls. This can take quite a while as their artists depicted the satanic tortures of the damned and martyred with the zeal of Hieronymos Bosch, and macabre images and imaginary beasties have a fascination the more usual New Testament scenes cannot match. Sorely conscious of the guardians' restive glares, I did not stay as long as I'd have liked.

I joined my husband in the café in the square, where he was the only non-local. We compared notes. He'd found out that while only 300 people live on the island, it boasts 580 registered voters. The same families have owned its 110 slate-roofed houses for generations and no one would ever dare sell to an outsider. They live off tourism and yet apart from the handful of fish-tank tavernas and silver shops, it is remarkably uncommercial. Sure, souvenirs are thrust at you when you file up the

Icicles consume a lakeside taverna during the freeze of January 2006

street from the dock. But they consist of samples of delectable sweets: flower-shaped crushed almond confections, honey-soaked pastries, gooey Turkish delight. You could make a meal from these handouts, the only hint of Anatolia on Nisi.

I confess we did not venture deep into modern Yannina. The archaeological museum, considered a masterpiece of contemporary architecture designed by Aris Konstantinidis, was shut for repairs. Besides, our waiter at Stin Ithaki had said, "Yannina is continually in the throes of a radical facelift. Stay away for a couple of years and even if you grew up here, you won't recognise a thing."

But some things endure: the castle, the lake and the ghost of Ali Pasha hovering around them. We got into the car to do the next thing that most tourists do after they've seen Yannina – head for the mountains. ⬤

How to get there

Flying to Yannina via Aegean or Olympic is the quickest option if all you want is a weekend change of scene. There's no need for a car in town and you can catch a bus to Dodoni.

Where to stay (area code 26510)

The *Hotel Kastro* (22866) inside the castle walls, next to Its Kaleh and the Byzantine Museum, has seven rooms in a beautifully restored 19th century home decorated in "Yianniotiko Neoclassic style". In town, the *Tourist* (26443) and the *Palladion* (25856) are relatively quiet and convenient.

Where to eat

The lakefront offers a rarity: delicious food in a splendid location at reasonable prices. Apart from the rotisseries at the start of taverna row, *Stin Ithaki* specialises in fabulous mezedes from Anatolia, while *Limni* is the place to go for fish and seafood. *Stin Ithaki* sometimes brings a chef from Istanbul to teach its staff how to prepare more of the exotic delicacies for which the city is famous. The only danger is that the menu is so tempting your eyes may be bigger than your stomachs.

Yannina's island tavernas are renowned for their trout, crayfish, eels and frogs legs. They now come from farms, not the great, green, greasy waters of the lake.

Dodoni (22 km south of Yannina)

The Oracle at Dodoni, second only to Delphi in importance, was the oldest in Greece. Here Zeus married the Great Goddess in one of her guises Dione, which simply means wife of Zeus, and set up house in a giant oak. The Oracle spoke through a curious combination of rustling leaves and the vibrations set off when the priests struck one of a series of bronze cauldrons that ringed the sacred tree. (Might they have sounded like "Om"?) So great was the Oracle's reputation that when the Christians sacked it, they also uprooted all the oak trees. Pyrrhos built the famous theatre in the 3rd century BC to seat 17,000 spectators (about 3,000 more than Epidaurus). A restoration programme means that the drama festival has been put on hold.

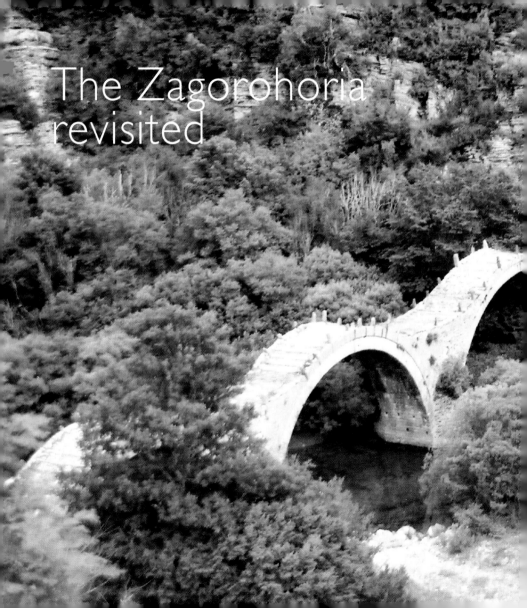

The Zagorohoria
revisited

We gritted our teeth and started to drag our bodies up this Golgotha but, half way to the top, Yorgos (a smoker in his 40s) flung himself on the flat stones and whispered that he'd rather die than go any further.

Y ou don't have to conquer the Vikos gorge to appreciate the Zagorohoria. These 46 Epirot villages, whose very name is said to mean "behind the mountains" in a Slavic dialect, lie in the Pindos range between Yannina, Metsovo and Konitsa. They have enough elegant stone bridges, houses, churches and awesome views visible from your car or within a few steps from it so that even a couch potato or a weak-kneed grandpa can drink in the beauty without overexerting himself. On the other hand, it's nice to be able to say you've done it.

The famous three-arched bridge at Kipi, one of the areas many musts

You don't need to conquer the Vikos gorge to appreciate its beauty

Some brochures maintain that the gorge – 12 km long, cut 1,200 m deep and between 100 and 1,000 m wide by the Voidomatis river – is the deepest in Europe. And while it may not be quite as spectacular as the Grand Canyon, plumbing its depths and scaling its heights is no mean feat. Eighteen years ago, in 1985 when the Zagori villages were just beginning to be rescued from decades of post-war abandonment, I set off with a group of about 15 friends from Athens for the sole purpose of walking the Vikos gorge, declared a national park 12 years earlier.

We spent the night in Yannina and next morning, before sunrise, boarded a hired minibus that ferried us to Monodendri, where

Some of the area's natural wonders are more accessible then others

we met our guide. The adventure began with a 30-minute climb straight down a ladder that eventually merged with steps carved into the cliffside. This was without doubt the worst part of the trek. I thought it would never end and, judging from the gasps and moans above and below me, many of my companions felt the same way. Stavros, at 62 our oldest member,

got stuck on a rung for several minutes, unable to go up or down. But eventually we reached bottom, not the bottom of the gorge but a goat path incised into what was still almost perpendicular wall. Take your eyes off your feet and you risked soaring into space.

At first the walk required so much concentration, we couldn't enjoy our surroundings, but

after a while we relaxed and looked for signs of life – the eagles, wild goats, deer and jackals that are meant to thrive here. Apart from birds, we saw nothing, but the rock formations, trees jutting from them, clusters of pink orchids and the immensity of it all kept us ecstatic. The high point of the trek must have been its lowest geographically: the Voidomati springs. There, azure water, clear as glass, collects in an enchanted pool ringed by silken sand and smooth boulders – the perfect balm for aching feet and sun-baked heads. Until the first toe ripples the surface. I'd never felt anything as cold, not in Maine, not in the Rockies. This was where we separated the men from the boys, or rather the women from the wimps. Because three of our party, all female, actually, managed a few strokes in the liquid ice; Koula, a former national backstroke champion, even swam across and back. Not one of the stronger sex even considered getting in over their ankles.

Women came out ahead, too, on the climb up out of the gorge. Here the path was an unrelenting series of stepped zigzags. We gritted our teeth and started to drag our bodies up

Megalo Papingo's little brother, Mikro Papingo, became wealthy during the Ottoman years by trading with eastern and central Europe

this Golgotha but, half way to the top, Yorgos (a smoker in his 40s) flung himself on the flat stones and whispered that he'd rather die than go any further. Coaxes and threats plus showers from our canteens finally got him moving again. Up to the outskirts of the village of Vikos, where water gushed from a wall and we soaked our heads back to normal. A pick-up was waiting to cart us to Papingo and we bid goodbye to our wonderful guide, who sprang up the side of the mountain and disappeared with a final wave, free at last to move at his own pace, faster than any goat.

The gorge walk had taken about six hours, not counting picnic, pool and recovery breaks. Was it worth it? Absolutely. We congratulated ourselves that night with dancing and singing, delectable Epirot pies as big as a hoplite's shield and gallons of beer and Zitsa wine. Then we passed out in soft beds under slate roofs in a couple of grey-stone houses converted with State loans into exemplary pensions.

The boost given then by the National Tourist Organisation was enough to turn Megalo (Big) Papingo into one of Greece's most de-

Oh my aching feet!

lightful, unblemished villages – in a class with Nymphaio, Ia, Makrynitsa, Ambelakia and Panormos on Tinos, with which it has formed an association. There's not an ugly building to be seen, no neon signs or plasticised photos serving as come-ons to its tavernas. Enormous plane trees cast dappled shade over squares and broad basilicas; roses tumble over every wall.

There is also a sense that money has been not only available but well spent in Papingo. This is not the case throughout the Zagori vil-

lages. Although almost all have benefited from the revival, many homes still stand empty. Collapsed walls are common, as are rickety padlocked gates barricading overgrown courtyards and worm-eaten timbers. Magnificent churches are crumbling, too. In tiny Koukouli, for example, the priest and his wife had joined forces with Albanian workers to pull down dangerous rotted beams in the village church which, along with its school and fountain house, is its most important landmark. Stunning frescoes of saints and the life of Christ shine out from their cobalt blue background, intricately carved beasts and garlands cover the templo, pulpit and priest's throne, but the priest doubted the money could be found to restore the building.

Monodendri, however, is a different story. Twenty years ago an unpretentious, perhaps even morose village, Monodendri has become the diva of Zagoria – a bit spoiled, a bit vulgar, showing off riches in rather questionable taste. Pullmans encircled the main square, but at least you still have to walk to the 15th century monastery of Agia Paraskevi, aka the Vikos Balcony, to get a proper view of the abyss. If you

Typical Zagorohoria square, this one belongs to Tsepelovo

Elegant stone bridges, houses, churches and awesome views are guaranteed throughout the area

really want your toes to curl, cross the three-plank "bridge" above it to a large cave on the other side of a smaller chasm that was used as a refuge from marauding Turks. From either vantage point, the view needs no embellishing, but 180 million drachmas (528,246 euros) were nevertheless lavished on paving the 600 metre-long path to the monastery in uneven white stone cobbles, which are neither pretty nor easy on the feet and ankles. The same white stones, so raw looking compared to the weathered brick-sized blocks used everywhere else, have been put to use in a similarly ostentatious open-air theatre near the start of the path.

A shepherd we met near the monastery, who was grazing his goats on the cliffside somewhere directly below us (!), filled our ears with local scandals. "My pension is only 210 euros a month, but my brother-in-law [a local official] bought a Mercedes you'd be ashamed to be seen in with kickbacks from the construction work." He wasn't the only one with a grievance. But then complaining about the establishment is a national sport in this country.

On the other hand, who could fault the projects sponsored by the Rizaris brothers, whose forefathers made a fortune in Moscow? The Rizarios Foundation, which runs an orphanage in Maroussi, has opened a boarding school in Monodendri, where up to 120 Albanian girls spend two years learning to weave traditional Epirot fabrics. Then they may choose between returning to Albania or living in Greece with IKA (social security) benefits; either way the foundation will buy their handiwork. In addition, the family mansion has been restored as an exhibition centre, and a chance to see the interior of a typical Zagori home.

Together with their scenery, the architecture in these villages – even when abandoned – sets them apart. The houses here are far from being humble rustic dwellings. Always built of local stone, with stern lines and a minimum of decoration, they blend impeccably with the surroundings, sometimes barely visible amidst thick forests. But they also proclaim a level of wealth and culture rarely found in such isolated settlements. We are accustomed to looking for civilisation in cities, *politismos stis poleis*. And yet, the people of Zagori turned their remoteness to advantage.

From as early as the 12th century they had to travel to make a living. By the 18th century, Zagorians had high positions in the Ottoman Empire and made sure their region was awarded privileges. At the same time, the money earned by merchants, jewellers, doctors or teachers in Romania, central Europe, Asia Minor and Russia paid not only for impressive houses but also for public schools, which even girls could attend, albeit separately. One man I met, who was setting up a photo exhibition in the schoolhouse in Koukouli, told me that the Golden Age of Epirus was 1750 to 1850, peaking during the reign of Ali Pasha, whose power and ambitions rivalled the Sultan's in this corner of the Ottoman Empire and kept the region free of brigands.

Now tourists are repopulating these remarkable villages, but the number of permanent residents is far lower than it was in their heyday. How ironic that in the era of SUVs, mobile phones and TV, it's harder to make a living in the mountains than it was 200 years ago. But even though many pensions are booked solid during holidays and on weekends, we needn't worry that the Zagoria will suffer the fate of Rhodes and Corfu. You'll find no drunken brawls here, just a pleasant camaraderie among fellow hikers in the tavernas after a day's walk (or drive) and welcoming smiles from the locals, all the wider if you can speak some Greek. ◯

How to get there

Yannina, the city closest to the Zagorohoria, can be reached by plane, car or bus. Having your own wheels is essential if you intend to explore but if all you want to do is hike, Trekking Hellas Epirus will arrange transportation to the Vikos gorge and other beauty spots. Contact them at Nap. Zerva 7-9, Yannina (26510 71703, fax 74190, epirus@trekking.gr). In Konitsa, No Limits can introduce you to any kind of mountain activity you can dream of from rafting and kayaking down the gorges, rappelling and canyoning in them or paragliding over them, tel. 26550 23777, fax 23548, info@nolimits.com.gr

Getting around

To simplify sightseeing by car, the most charming/interesting villages seem to be grouped into three clusters. The distances are small if mostly vertical, so it doesn't really matter where you're based. One route, from Metamorfosi on the main Konitsa-Yannina road, will take you to Dilofo and Kipi, then north to Koukouli, Kapesovo, Vradeto, where stone stairs curl like old-fashioned ringlets down to the bottom of the gorge, and Tsepelovo, with its handsome square. The middle route goes to Vitsa, one of the most harmonious of the villages, and Monodendri, while the north fork links Ano and Kato Pedina with a dirt road to Aristi, where asphalted again it climbs to Megalo and Mikro Papingo. Above Monodendri at Oxia, another "balcony", the gorge is lined with extravagant stone pillars looking as though they've been lifted from Angkor Wat and magnified a thousand times. Almost every village has signed paths to other villages, while three hours of walking will get you from Papingo to Drakolimni, the largest lake in the Vikos National Park. There is no off-season in the Zagorohoria, but don't attempt the major hikes without a guide or in bad weather.

Where to stay (area code 26530)

Hotel *Ameliko*, Ano Pedina (71501); Guest House *Koukouli*, Koukouli (71070); and in Yannina, Hotel *Kastro*, Andr. Paleologou 57 (26510 22866). These three small hotels are run by the same people and are notable for their charm, cleanliness and price. They have the same e-mail address: rit-zan@otenet.gr. *Xenonas Dias*, Mikro Papingo, (41257 & 41892). Twelve rooms in two traditional buildings with a taverna and courtyard in between. *Xenonas tou Kouli*, Papingo, tel.-fax 41115, pretty rooms adjoining a pleasant café. *Arhontiko tis Aristis*, Aristi (42210), two stone houses, one dates to 1800, the other new but in the same style, fabulous views and atmosphere, with restaurant; *Orestes' House*, Ano Pedina (71202), cosy and casual hikers' favourite; *Papaevangelou Guest House*, Megalo Papingo (41135), family-run rooms and cottages, a jewel; *Saxoni's Houses*, Megalo Papingo (41615), simple and peaceful at the quiet end of the village; *Dias Guest House*, Mikro Papingo (41257), another trekkers' choice, another extraordinary setting and courtyard taverna. All these small hotels combine warm hospitality with stunning locations.

Where to eat

Dias Guest House, *Ta Panta Rei* in Koukouli, and *Michali's taverna* in Kipi all serve local specialities like cheese and greens pies, baked feta, *galotiri* (a fresh, slightly sour, soft cheese) and Zitsa wine. Michali's also makes a fine *kokkora krasato* (rooster in wine sauce) with a bird so big (but so tasty) we thought it was turkey, and homemade *baklava* and *kataifi*. Be careful when ordering trout, another local speciality; it can be treacherously bony if too small.

Some houses like this
are now cosy hotels

Exploring Tzoumerka

Something had to be done with all that wool, so while half the population were shepherds, the other half made capes. They were such good quality they were in demand all over Europe.

"Did you know that the capes worn by Napoleon's Grand Army were made here?"

We're sitting on an eagle's nest of a terrace in the village of Syrrako, facing a panorama of snow-covered mountains sharp as shark's teeth. Yannina may lie only 40 km away but it feels like we're somewhere beyond the edge of the world now, in the 21st century. How could this rock-bound little place have had dealings with Paris two hundred years ago?

In fact, we're still recovering from our traumatic drive here. The road, though mostly asphalted, climbed relentlessly into the mountains,

This being Epirus, no location is without its stone bridge. Now as deserted as its surroundings, the Plaka bridge was once a major thoroughfare

Kipina monastery, well hidden in a cleft in the rocks

giving us stomach-churning glimpses of vein-like rivers at the bottom of impossibly deep gorges and inspiring vistas of Tzoumerka's towering peaks. Until today, my only contact with these mountains in the central Pindos had been a taverna by that name on the back side of Parnitha where Athenians go to eat lamb chops on Sundays.

Our nerves held steady until we came to what looked like a war monument built on the side of an especially tight hairpin bend. It marked the spot where a bus carrying 29 villagers plunged into the abyss a few decades ago. We gulped but resisted the impulse to rush back to Yannina. Alone on the road, we passed thick fir forests that perfumed the air

Kalarites was once a village of silversmiths

with Christmas, a pink villa on stilts and a tattered banner wishing visitors Chronia Polla (the traditional holiday greeting) at the entrance to an invisible hamlet called Kedros. A long stretch of tumbled rocks and scree left us trembling and now I thought I knew why our friends in Yannina had said, "You'll have an interesting time getting to Syrrako."

Rounding the upteenth zigzag, we finally saw the village – a tidy cluster of grand stone mansions that defied gravity by remaining glued to the precipitous, tree-studded mountainside. It looked like the port of Hydra transmogrified to the Alps. We parked the car where the road stopped and waited for Panayiotis Dodouros, the owner of our hotel, to fetch us in his jeep.

The Arachthos river, ideal for rafting

"Are you sure we're all right here?" we asked. "What about the bus stop sign?"

"Oh, that's just wishful thinking," he replied with a grin. "No bus has stopped here in years."

We rattled over a bumpy track to the outskirts of upper Syrrako, where Panayiotis' wife Popi was waiting. It was a short walk to her family home, which she opened as a small hotel in 2001. She calls it Kasa Kalda, which means warm house in Vlachika. All the villages in this part of Tzoumerka were founded by Koutsovlach nomadic shepherds from Thessaly in the 14th and 15th centuries, when to stay in the plains meant unpleasant confrontations with the Turks.

Which brings us back to that question of Napoleon's capes. "You see," says Popi, her dark curls bobbing with enthusiasm, "we have 36,000 *stremmata* (9,000 acres) of pasture up here. In the old days, they used to feed 50,000 to 60,000 sheep. Something had to be done with all that wool, so while half the population were shepherds, the other half made capes. They were such good quality they were in demand all over Europe."

"But how did they get there?"

"On the backs of mules down to Preveza and then onto ships that would take them to the Black Sea and up the Adriatic. Even though they were mountain people, Syrrako and Kalarites (the nextdoor village) had their own ships. Both our biggest churches are dedicated to St. Nicholas, the patron saint of sailors."

This is about as strange as finding a chapel to Prophet Elijah in a valley near the sea. Stranger still is the discovery that Kalarites had been renowned for its silversmiths and that the Bulgari jewellery dynasty of Rome had originated there (though it's not the only place in Epirus to claim this distinction).

Nowadays, sadly, both villages are practically deserted in winter. "Everyone comes back for the 15th of August," says Popi. "Maybe 3,000 or so people, from Preveza and Yannina mostly. Emigration started here with liberation, in 1913, but no one actually left the country. Life is hard, we're practically snowbound from January to April. Ten years ago Syrrako was totally abandoned. Even now in the worst months there are only about three or four of us here, besides Panayiotis and me. But there are signs that things are changing. All the *kaldcrimia* have new cobbles, we have a new water supply system and we even have a Citizens' Assistance office. So maybe we'll get a few more citizens."

We sit on Popi's terrace sipping mountain tea until the sun slips behind a cloud. She's created four or five sitting areas under fruit trees, flowering vines cling to the white stone bricks of the house, and pots with more flowers occupy every step and ledge.

"You have green fingers," I say.

Popi replies, "Even if I didn't, I'd need the plants for colour, to break up all this stone."

Inside the three-storey house, built in 1864, the colour comes from traditional bedspreads, cushions and rugs. Red and black plaids predominate, sometimes enlivened with bold splashes of pink or smaller white, pink and grey embroidery. We sit in the cosy *katogi* or cellar and switch to tsipouro, a wintry drink befitting the occasion. Rain has just started to pelt down.

But Panayiotis predicts it won't last. When it stops, Popi offers to guide us downtown to the taverna ("You'd never find it on your own".).

The tour starts near the top of the village at the church of the Panayia Theotokou. Popi points out a little round face stamped onto the belltower – the mark of the master builder. "In the past every building had one. You just have to look." Then she told us that the church was built by two cape-merchant brothers, as a means of atonement when one finally confessed to the other he'd been stealing from his share of the profits.

"And here is where the town crier used to stand and announce the news or the arrival, let's say, of the miller with bags of flour to sell."

As we trail down the cobbled paths, Popi brings the village back to life. At the church of St. Nicholas, she shows us where three groups of young people would dance under the two plane trees in the square surrounding it. "During the *panigyri* the older women would sit there, on the ledge above, gossiping and matchmaking. I forgot to tell you about the horse traders. Before they set off, the hills would be black with horses. They would herd them all the way to Romania and sell them in exchange for paprika."

Popi deposits us at the upper taverna, clearly spurning Syrrako's second taverna across the narrow street, which looks almost identical. Next to it, a digital clock/thermometer blinks yellow numbers inside a dark fountain house. No one can explain how this modern intrusion got there. Evrydiki, both cook and waitress, serves us tender lambchops that taste like the real thing, a medley of juicy overstuffed vegetables and delicious white wine. Before we know

it, Panayiotis appears to lead us through the cobbled maze back to Kasa Kalda.

The next morning, we are not alone at breakfast. Four more couples have arrived in the night, cross country from Thessaloniki. Popi pulls out all the stops and breakfast keeps coming: bread with local honey and butter, two kinds of homemade cake, followed by two kinds of pie, hot from the oven, a sweet custard without a crust and a savoury cheese creation called simply "zymaropita" or dough pie. All of us women whip out pencils and paper for the recipe.

It's time to go but no one can bear to leave. Finally Panayiotis says he'll take our bags down to the car and Popi will guide us through the village to the lower road. We all traipse behind her, through the little park with busts of famous natives like Kolettis, Ali Pasha's physician, who went on to become a prime minister; a folk art collection in the home of poet Kostas Krystallis; the old school, far and away Syrrako's largest building; and the orphanage, both of which are now hotels. I kiss Popi and Panayiotis goodbye, making plans to come back and walk the path down the cliff and back up the other side to Kalarites, which Popi says is beautiful and not too arduous.

Today we have to drive there, but not even this road, which has been sliced into the precipice, can spook us now, though looking

Waterfalls are common in Tzoumerka

back down at where we've come from does provoke a mild dizzy spell. And that creaky wooden bridge over a bottomless gorge does not inspire confidence either. Still the cuckoos are chiming, the wooded slopes opposite look smooth as velvet, flowers spangle the roadside and all's right with the world.

Like Syrrako, Kalarites has no cars or motorbikes, so we park by a spring and walk. Another sonnet in stone, this village is more strung out than its neighbour, less orderly but more lived in. It's also more colourful. Plane and linden trees break up the continuity of grey stone and slate roofs, pink and blue flokatis hang from windowsills, and about a dozen people are sitting in the café.

They're shepherds from Tyrnavo in Thessaly. In time-honoured tradition, they've brought their sheep up here to pasture from May to October. But the flocks have dwindled to between 12,000 and 15,000 head and they arrive in pickups. Long gone are the days of the massive migrations on foot and, thanks to their wheels, the men can enjoy chatting in the café and a bit of family life by day. By twilight, though, they're back at the pastures to take care of the animals. Most of these shepherds look at least sixty; only one is in his thirties. They may be the last of a vanishing breed. As for the silversmiths, they've disappeared with the capemakers.

We spend the rest of the day doing the Tzoumerka circuit of special landmarks. Tucked into a slit in the cliff face above the Kalarites river, the Kipina monastery blends so well into the pale beige rocks you hardly know it's there. The date carved next to the door reads 1212. Freshly watered flower pots hint at inhabitants but no one answers my knocks.

We pass several hamlets of varying degrees of charm. Ktistades, named for its master builders, is a disgrace to its founders. The new generation has replaced the original stone houses with cement cottages shouting their modernity with red tile roofs and aluminium doors. Fortunately, it is an exception.

Pramanta deserves attention as Tzoumerka's biggest village but Syrrako and Kalarites have left us satiated so we head for its cave instead. Although it was discovered in 1961, Pramanta's cavern was not opened to the public until 2003. A young couple has the concession for the taverna at its entrance as well as the visits. We like their role-switching: Christos does the cooking, while Chryssoula takes you underground.

If you are only mildly enthusiastic about delving into the bowels of the earth, this is the cave for you. Its 300 m of exuberant sculpture require a mere 10-15 minutes of your time. You even get double your money because all

of its stalactites – phalluses, fancied resemblances and ogival arches – are reflected in a string of lovely still, reddish pools.

This being Epirus, a stone bridge is next on the agenda. We find the sign at the Arachthos river bed – Historic Bridge of Plaka and Holly Monastery – but all we see is a wooden bridge and a half-finished Trekking Hellas rafting camp. Were it not for an elderly shepherdess, we would have abandoned the search.

Wearing thick black wool stockings, a heavy dark blue skirt, apron and head scarf, she bares her four teeth in a sort of smile and launches into a tale of woe. She's one of two old people left in the village. Her fields have run wild, and there's no one to shear her sheep. Oblivious to the flies tacked to her mahogany arm, she points us in the direction of an overgrown path.

In about ten hot, sticky minutes, we're climbing over a magnificent, almost circular arch 40 m above the river. Unlikely as it seems now, this was one of the border crossings between free Greece and the Ottoman Empire until 1913.

Once so populous and prosperous, Tzoumerka is just beginning to attract visitors. But I predict that it will not be long before its mountains, villages, caves and gorges are as full of adventurers as the Zagorohoria to the north. ○

How to get there

For this route you need a car, preferably a 4X4 if you want to go off the asphalt. Syrrako is only about 40 km south of Yannina. It just feels further. Like the Zagoria, Tzoumerka has 47 villages, so this circuit is just a tiny taste of what the region has to offer.

Syrrako (above and below) - poetry in stone

Where to stay

In Syrrako, there are three small hotels, but *Kasa Kalda* (*Bitsios Lodge*) is by far the most charming. (26510 53540). There are also a few small guesthouses in Kalarites and Pramanta, the biggest village in the region, has a hotel called *Tzoumerka* (26590 61336).

Where to eat

Be sure you choose the upper tavernaki in Syrrako; it is by far the more congenial. Outside Pramanta, the *Cave* is a fine place to stop before or after visiting it. *Christos Vourlokas* prepares simple homey dishes.

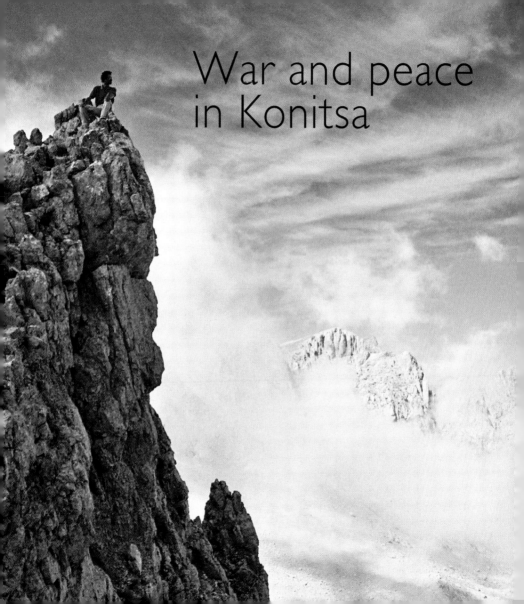

War and peace
in Konitsa

We'd thought of looking for a room in one of the *mastorohoria* the road has just passed through. With no resources except stone, these villages produced the master masons and other craftsmen who are said to have "built the world".

The grassy uplands of Mt Gamila, with the peaks of Astraka looking on menacingly

We're driving from Kastoria to Epirus through some of the most spectacular scenery Greece has to offer. Thick forests of evergreens, oaks and chestnuts spread over steep hills, boulders that rival Meteora's in shape if not in size sprawl beneath villages hewn from the same material. Water pours out of the rocks as we enter Epirus and cross the muddy Sarantaporos river for the first of many times. A large billboard informs us that the bridge here, out of commission since the Italians bombed it in 1943, was rebuilt at the turn of this century with EU funds.

Breathtaking though the road is, night is falling and my husband mutters, "One of the things I vowed I'd never do was to drive in Epirus anywhere near the Albanian border and here I am doing just that." There is nothing overtly threatening or risky about our circumstances, but the Pindos is perhaps the bloodiest, most war-scarred district in all Greece. And we are well aware that Mt. Grammos to our right is still studded with mines and the only people you'd be likely to encounter there at night are Albanian mafiosi.

We'd thought of looking for a room in one of the *mastorohoria* the road has just passed through. With no resources except stone, these villages produced the master masons and other craftsmen who are said to have "built the world". While this is obviously something of an exaggeration, starting in the 18th century teams of men from Pentalofos and Eptahori in Mace-

Pentalofos (on its five hills) as "a poem". But unlike the Zagori villages further south, handsome as they are, these settlements are not used to visitors and the one tiny hotel we stumbled upon looked less than spotless and very noisy. (I later learned that Pyrsoyianni has a pleasant *xenona* or inn and a photo exhibition of early 20th century immigrants to Ellis Island on permanent view that is very touching.)

So here we are, getting ever closer to the Albanian border, which at dusk is beginning to seem increasingly like the twilight zone. But another guidebook (*Only the Best, Greece*) suggests what could be our salvation: "Hotel Bourazani. Built of wood and stone, discreetly decorated and furnished, isolated in its private park bisected by the Aoos river... 20 rooms. Fantastic restaurant." I call to make sure there's a room available and suddenly the darkening trees and winding road lose their spookiness, despite the lack of traffic. Eventually we begin to spot its signs and follow them into even more remote woods illuminated by sporadic bursts of sheet lightning.

Surrounded by rose bushes and verandas,

donia and Pyrsoyianni, Vourbiani and other hamlets in Epirus set off every spring for distant corners of Greece and even Asia Minor. From the Peloponnese to Thrace, Thessaly – think of Pelion – and such towns in the north as Nymphaio, you can't miss the finely chiselled grey-stone churches, houses and public buildings that are their trademark. Somehow they also found time to carve out masterpieces in their own villages, and our guidebook extols

The snow-streaked uplands of Mt Gamila (Tymfi) in early June,
with the crags of Astrakas peak behind

the pale ochre two-storey hotel looks worlds away from the *mastorohoria*. We park near the swimming pool and step into a spacious, wood-panelled hunting lodge. Trophies of big game hunters – antlers, stuffed stag heads and the like – decorate the walls, immaculate white-napped tables set for a hundred diners fill the much-touted restaurant, but we seem to be the only guests. The owner, a businesslike older woman, assures us that the place is a favourite with foreigners and groups drawn by the hotel's 300-acre wildlife park and eco-centre, where deer, boar, jackals and other creatures roam free. "The animals wake up in the evening so we run

The Drakolimni on Mt Gamila, as the last snowpack melts into the tarn

the grounds. Here, too, we are the only customers but at least it's informal and we can chat to the proprietors while we feast on grilled trout plucked from a tank on their terrace. The lightning continues to flare up the sky but they win the bet that it won't rain. They, and indeed everyone we meet in the area, also tell us that "the Albanians give us no trouble here. The army is close by, for one thing, and they head for the cities where they can make more money."

In the morning, leaving the hotel and driving even further west into the mountains, we see just how close the army is. As we ascend through verdant countryside spangled with yellow, blue, white and pink flowers and creepers, a multi-laned border crossing, cleared of all vegetation, stands out in the river valley below, flanked by an impressive array of military vehicles. In contrast, the first village we come to, Aidonohori, looks extremely peaceful, even modestly prosperous, with attractive new houses sprinkled between older buildings and a 19th century basilica that dwarfs them all. Locals in its little café say sixty people live here permanently.

The Panayia Molivdoskepasti, back down in the valley, is the region's most prized monument. Taking its name from the lead sheets in its roof, this exquisite monastery was founded

our minibus safaris between 7 and 9 in the summer. You've missed today's so you'll have to spend another night. Lots of our guests use this as a base for exploring the Zagorohoria." We tell her we'll think about it.

After plopping our bags in our comfortable room, we sneak out to the taverna just outside

Started in 1823, this bridge below Konitsa, at 20m high, 42m wide, is reputedly the largest span in the Balkans

in the 7th century, where the Aoos and Sarantaporos rivers meet. It must have been restored since then, but its tall dome and blooming courtyard look in mint condition. Some of the books on sale have intriguing titles: *Pos einai i Kolasi, Pos einai o Paradeisos* – or roughly translated, "what hell and heaven are like"! Written from personal experience no doubt.

Now we're ready to tackle Konitsa, the only town in this district. Terra incognita. I know only two things about it: it was the scene of a decisive siege during the Civil War and Queen Frederika, ex-King Constantine's mother, liked to troutfish nearby. From a distance, it's just a blip at the foot of three of the mightiest peaks in the Pindos – Grammos, Smolikas and Gamila – a mundane market centre overlooking a fertile valley, velvety green hills and darker clusters of trees.

On this bright June day the Christmas holidays of 1947 are almost impossible to conjure up, not just because of their freezing temperatures. After an uneasy truce of more than two years, the suppressed tensions and resentments between Nationalists and Communists were bubbling closer and closer to all-out war, especially in the north of Greece. On December 23, the Communists proclaimed Konitsa capital of their Provisional Democratic Government. All that remained was to capture it and that must have seemed easy enough with their 2,200 troops pitched against the 400 Nationalist soldiers left to defend the place, some 900 having been granted leave. The Communists attacked on Christmas Day, taking the townspeople and the country by surprise. Secretly, the Communists had brought in heavy weapons and plenty of ammunition from Albania and they quickly took control of the roads between Konitsa and the outside world.

For the next twelve days, the regular troops with the dogged support of the Konitsans somehow succeeded in preventing the Communists from entering the town, despite losing key positions at higher spots to the north and their commanding officer to a landmine. But they were running out of food and ammunition and could not have held out had not the Communists, perhaps exhausted themselves, called off or shifted the focus of their attacks on two occasions. Just before 8 pm on New Year's Eve, when the Nationalists were on the point of giving up, reinforcements arrived against unbelievable odds. An infantry battalion, accompanied by a squadron of gendarmerie, had followed mountain paths from Yannina, fording flooded streams and fighting off pockets of guerrillas, to arrive muddy and bedraggled at the southern entrance to town, the Stomio bridge – the stone bridge with the highest arch in Epirus. Six hours later a band of Special Forces straggled in, further boosting morale but only lightly armed.

By the 6th of January, thanks to the arrival of more reinforcements, ammunition and supplies, the battle for Konitsa was over. The Communists retreated, taking their fight back to the mountains, which they would not give up for another two years. They lost prestige with sympathisers abroad, while for the Army and the Nationalists back in Athens, Konitsa became a landmark victory, proving that with determination the Communists could be defeated.

The very next day, January 7, Queen Frederika travelled from Yannina by jeep over mined roads still bristling with sharpshooters to congratulate the people of Konitsa on their extraordinary bravery. King Paul, who had only that year come to the throne, lay ill with typhoid in Athens. A British officer, Michael Ward, inspecting Konitsa conditions for UNSCOB (UN Special Committee for the Balkans), happened to meet her. "Her eyes were bloodshot from fatigue, her face covered with mud slicks, and her heavy shoes and lisle stockings caked with mire. We introduced ourselves quickly and made to leave, but the queen, in spite of being tired out from a 9-hour round trip over appalling roads, coupled with the emotional experience of her ovation in Konitsa, insisted on inviting us to enter and sit down. Turning to [her lady in waiting], she said, 'Mary, I think we still have a bottle of Scotch vitamins left. Could you please bring it? I would like to share it with my visitors.'"

Frederika was to become a controversial figure, but even her detractors could not deny her courage that winter day. Perhaps her welcome then made the area's trout streams that much more appealing when the war was over.

Konitsa today shows no battle scars. Its 5,000 inhabitants are so laid back they don't even honk their horns or make a fuss when someone leaves their car or pickup idling in mid-street while he or she runs off to do an errand. Though in no way "a poem" like the villages of Zagori or the *mastorohoria*, it does have a few memorable structures like the bridge, of course, and the fortress-like mansion Ali Pasha built for his mother, Hamko.

But anything man-made would pale next to this district's natural wonders, and one organisation has redefined Konitsa as the extreme sports capital of Greece. Its name is No Limits and it operates in an anonymous building just off the main square. Headed by Nikos Kyritsis, who at forty has shrugged off stories of the divisive past, the energetic young staff guides groups of varying sizes on expeditions all year round. With No Limits you can test your skills and nerves at rafting, canyonning, kayaking, paragliding, mountain biking, bungee jumping, skiing (at Vasilitsa to the southeast), and of course trekking. Besides the celebrated Vikos gorge, the Voidomati and Aoos gorges are less demanding but also stunningly beautiful. For the less energetic, there are jeep safaris into Smolikas and Grammos and tours of the *mastorohoria*.

The Vikos is not the only gorge

Every year, since 1996, No Limits attracts extreme sports fans (or masochists, depending on your point of view) for a series of championship events known as Evathlos held over three days in June. In 2003 the rafting event crossed over into Albania in a gesture of friendship. It gives me hope that men and women are playing in mountains that only a few decades ago saw unimaginable horrors and atrocities. Then they did extreme things because their lives depended on it. Now blessed with time, money and peace, we do them only because we want to. ○

How to get there

The Konitsa area is in the northwest corner of Epirus, not far from the Albanian border. To explore properly it is essential to have a car, but if you don't want to drive all the way from Athens or Thessaloniki, you can fly to Yannina and rent a car there.

Where to stay

Hotel *Bourazani*, about 20 minutes west of Konitsa (22650 61283, fax 61321, burazani@otenet.gr)

In Konitsa, there are more than a dozen small hotels and rooms to rent. No Limits recommends the *Gefyri*, *Artemis*, *Hani* and *Grand Dendro* (sic) as well as their own *Phaedon rooms* and suggests you reserve through them and get the bonus of discounted prices. No Limits also runs a hotel in Aristi, where they offer a special weekend package of activities.

Where to eat

The taverna just before the turn to the Bourazani hotel serves delicious trout fresh from their tank. The hotel itself is famous for game dishes and its wine list, and friends have dined happily there.

In Konitsa, *Angeliki Papamichail's* small shop on the main square sells local products, including a superb aubergine relish, a wide variety of liqueurs, honey, spoon sweets and homemade noodles.

Sports and hiking contacts

No Limits, The Outdoor Experience, Konitsa (26550 23777, fax 23548, info@nolimits. com.gr)

Trekking Hellas Epirus, Nap. Zerva 7-9, Yannina (26510 71703, fax 74190, epirus@ trekking.gr)

Kastoria

Kastoria earned its name from the beavers that once flourished there and gave rise to a major fur trade – now storks wade in the shallows

efore I set out for Kastoria, one or two old-timer friends shook their heads knowingly and said, "Poh, poh, the city's ruined. Nothing but cement wherever you look, and cars… the locals wouldn't walk two blocks if their lives depended on it." Now that I've been there, I beg to differ. This town on a lake in western Macedonia may not be the Venice of the North, but it certainly ranks as one of Greece's most delightful small cities, on a par with Nafplion, Corfu, Xanthi and Ermoupolis.

Glimpsed from afar, it could be an artist's rendition of a dreamscape: a gently undulating peninsula, studded with white facades, red roofs and bursts of dark green trees, afloat in shimmering water, with ducks and grebes bobbing in the foreground. The setting could hardly be improved upon, and the lake's changing moods infuse Kastoria with a light, open quality unusual in the interior. At this distance, you can almost imagine the sight that greeted the first settlers, a tribe called the Orestes, said to have descended from Agamemnon's vengeful son. In their honour, the lake is still called Orestiada. Though they named their own town Keletron, the word Kastoria most probably derives from the lake's even earlier inhabitants, the beavers, *kastores*, whose pelts were to launch Kastorians in a profession that would make them rich and famous.

Living in such a cold climate, the locals must have wrapped themselves in fur from the start, but by the 15th century they started to specialise in stitching scraps together into apparently seamless coats and capes. As whole pelts became scarce, it was this talent, which is not practiced in other fur-producing areas, that won them renown and customers first from Vienna to Stockholm, later New York, but always Moscow. The Russian connection is obvious for miles outside town. Signs in Cyrillic direct salesmen to the fur manufacturers, large hotels and exhibition rooms that line the main road. Fur sales to the west – the US, Scandinavia and Germany – fell in the 1980s when political correctness took precedence over warmth, but in post-perestroika Russia there were no such objections. Sadly for Kastoria, the collapse of the ruble in 1998 put lots of the city's furriers out of work. Even so, furs account for a whopping 43 percent of Greece's exports to Russia.

But I'm getting ahead of myself. By Justinian's time, Kastoria was a jewel in the Byzantine crown, and you can still see sections of the wall he had built to defend it – near the Town Hall and the stadium – from Slavs pressing southward. Later invaders toppled the walls, and Kastoria changed hands repeatedly, as Bulgarians, Normans, Serbs and Albanians challenged Byzantium's rule. In 1385, all competition ceased when the Turks took over what they called Sach Giol or "Royal Lake"; they stayed in charge until 1912.

Despite centuries of strife and repeated regime change, Kastoria prospered. And its citizens engaged in another of their favourite pastimes: building churches. Depending on which guidebook you read, this town of only 18,000 inhabitants boasts 70 to 80 Byzantine and Post-Byzantine churches. Most of them are small, erected as private chapels by prominent families, neighbourhoods or guilds, and they are scattered throughout the town, like raisins in a loaf, sometimes four or five on a single street.

What is shocking is that only five of them are visitable. The rest are firmly locked and in dire need of restoration, according to our guide from the Byzantine Museum. The museum itself, near the highest point in town, is another scandal. It houses one of the world's finest collections of icons, comparable with those of Mount Athos and St. Catherine's monastery in Sinai, and yet only 37 of the 500 in its possession are on display. As our guide said, "There are just no funds for conservation, for the icons, the churches, or even for this building," which is rundown and badly lit, with paint flapping from the walls. "Promises are made every election year, but no money ever comes our way."

Nevertheless, the icons and altar doors radiate from their drab prison and each of the five churches, within a 30-minute walk, conceals something unique behind its intricate brickwork. The Panayia Kombelidiki, recognisable by its tall priest's-hat dome, has a fresco above the door of Salome dancing as she balances the platter

The Panayia Kombelidiki
has a fresco depicting
Salome's dance

hundreds of orders for fur coats and fine jewellery (another Kastorian talent) stand in every conceivable state of disrepair. In the saddest cases, only the thick stone walls of the ground floor remain intact, a receptacle for the wooden beams, *hayiatia* (enclosed protruding balconies), plaster and stained glass that have collapsed into them. Others have clearly been abandoned for blocks of flats, while many that are still occupied cannot be pleasant to live in. No doubt this is what those old timers back in Athens were tut-tutting about.

However, enough masterpieces exist in mint or semi-mint condition to spellbind and utterly charm the visitor. They are concentrated in two neighbourhoods, Apozari on the north shore and Doltso, from the top of the hill down to the lake on the south shore. Doltso is a Vlach word akin to *dolce*, meaning sweet; and life here must have been sweet indeed one or two centuries ago when the world was clamouring for Kastoria's furs.

Many of the houses near the lake have lawns and gardens, from which roses tumbled on our June visit. As we walked up and down

with St. John the Baptist's head on her own; the Taxiarchis contains the tombs of Macedonian freedom fighter Pavlos Melas and his wife Natalia, while Agios Athanasios, only recently opened to the public, is covered with frescoes of the saints wearing elaborate headgear instead of halos.

Even more noticeable than the churches is Kastoria's distinctive architecture. And here again you mourn the lack of funds for restoration. The three-storey mansions representing the cobbled streets, littered only by the occasional tuft of fur, we stopped to watch a man in his garden staple together rectangular scraps of mink onto a large plywood board, as though he were designing a jigsaw puzzle. He told us it might take a good worker only one day to stitch these hundreds of little pieces together into strips and then sew the strips with invisible threads into a luxurious coat. Despite the depressed market, the furriers are still hard at work. Peer into a window, and in all probability you'll see a row of sewing machines and men bent over pelts of fur late into the evening. Our new friend invited us to have a look at his house when his wife returned; we lingered but eventually ambled away, not wishing to impose.

Also in Doltso, a few hundred metres from the lake, the Aivazi mansion has been restored as an engaging folklore museum – and satisfies a voyeur's curiosity about what transpires behind those intriguing walls. With Eftyhios Ballis guiding you through every nook and cranny, you come away with a good sense of what Kastoria home life could have been like up to 60 years ago. First of all, you could have fished off the balcony – the lake was higher then – and paddled out into it in your *kravi*, a gondola-like craft. In winter you'd have sat next to the beautiful moulded fireplace, sun shining through 17th century stained glass and casting rainbows over the intri-

cate paintings on the panelled walls opposite. If a prospective suitor happened to call, you could have inspected him from behind a screened peephole, and given the word to serve him sugarless coffee if he didn't meet your approval, sweet coffee and *tsipouro* if you'd decided to accept his attentions. Has Ballis had any State help in maintaining this showplace? The old man laughed, "The State doesn't give me a cent, but they always bring VIPs to admire it."

Another, unexpected, attraction of Kastoria is how much of the peninsula is unbuilt. As abruptly as Dolto's lakeshore tavernas, homes and playgrounds end, thick forest starts, interrupted very infrequently by a chapel. The drive lazes around the coast, past fishermen and women (even at night in the rain), joggers, kids on bikes and in strollers. How many other Greek cities have had the restraint and good sense to leave their greenery intact? Kastoria has also cleaned up the lake; Ballis said the water was drinkable, not just a sanctuary for dozens of bird species.

Easing the transition between "country" and city on the north side of the peninsula is a Kastoria landmark, the brilliant white monastery of Panayia tis Mavriotissas and the church of Agios Ioannis o Theologos. More than the grisly depictions of the Last Judgement in the latter's frescoes, I suspect the main allure is sitting in

Only a few of Kastoria's fine old mansions are still private homes – many are too ruined for repair

the pleasant lakeside café next door under the huge plane trees and watching the pelicans whirl overhead.

Yes, there is too much cement in the centre of town just minutes away, where traffic comes to a standstill, especially on market day. Yes, more could be done to restore the city's precious icons, churches and houses, but for the moment Kastoria remains the pearl of Macedonia.

Don't leave Kastoria without visiting the an-cient site and small museum at Dispilio, at the southern edge of the lake. You will find no temple foundations or marble columns, but rather clay huts, reed roofs and dugout canoes. This was the site of the oldest lake settlement yet discovered in Europe. Way back around 5500 BC, some 3,000 hunters and fishers and their families lived here on platforms built on chestnut poles sunk into the mud. The poles, which had not rotted in all those millennia,

Kastoria's first settlers lived in reed huts on the lake some 7,500 years ago

showed up first in 1932, when the water level receded during a great drought, and again in 1965. But excavations only began in 1992. From the sludge, archaeologists managed to reconstruct an idea of the village, which stretched 4.5 km, and have built a few model dwellings on the basis of their finds. One, with an animal skull above the door, represents the shaman's hut. The settlers were resourceful, fishing with obsidian spearheads and bone hooks, nets made of animal gut, and reed traps. They also had devised a form of writing that looks a bit like Linear A and played tunes on a flute made of a bird's bone – very advanced for their time. They were Pygmy height (1.30 m), had a life expectancy of 25 to 30 years, and after a couple of thousand years they burned their village, and moved on. They left no trace. Visitable since April 2000, their reconstructed homes are surely unique among Greece's antiquities. ○

How to get there

Kastoria does have an airport but we drove there via Lamia, Karditsa, Kalambaka, and Grevena in about 5 hours plus a stop for a picnic in the beautiful hills before Grevena.

Where to stay (area code 24670)

We stayed at the very comfortable B class *Kastoria Hotel*, on the north shore of the peninsula near the Yacht Club (29453). Other hotels that come highly recommended are *To Archontiko tis Venetoulas*, B class, 8 rooms in a restored 1920s house in the Doltso district (22446); and *Vergoula's Mansion* (23415), a 19th century beauty with enormous beds and bedrooms facing the lake and furniture from the Balkans and the East.

Where to eat

The locals like to eat grilled meat at *To Tzaki* and *To Hayiati* in the green village of Ambelokipi, west of town off the road to Kozani. But there are plenty of delightful tavernas along the lake shore drive. We tried *Krondiri*, on the south side near Doltso, dining on snail casserole, mushroom soufflé and baked apple, which are only some of their local specialities. The wine is invariably good red Amynteo.

The Byzantine Museum, Dexameni Sq. near the old *Xenia* Hotel, is open from 8:30 am to 3 pm, closed Mondays and holidays (24670 26781). The Dispilio site is open daily 9 am to 1 pm.

Prespes: bean kingdom on the lakes

Serene and drowsy though it may seem now, this corner of Greece was not always at the end of the road. During the Byzantine years, long before the erection of national boundaries, Serbs and Bulgars as well as Greeks fought to build churches here and knocked down each other's castles.

The first thing that strikes you as you enter the Prespes Lake District is not the expanse of water, the flocks of pelicans or the hosts of wildflowers for which it is famous. Instead, all you see is fields of neat rows of beans. Stretching for miles in every direction, even the newly planted fields are equipped with beanpoles, standing in their thousands like tepees without a cover. There are whole forests of them, for Prespes must be the bean capital of this legume-loving country, where *fasolada* is the national dish. Instead of souvenirs, vendors sell sacks of beans at key locations where tourists come to look at birds. Giant beans; red, white, brown and black beans; and even jars of bean *glyko* or spoon sweet!

After driving here from Kastoria, over winding, narrow roads through fir-covered mountains with not a village in sight, these farms come as a complete surprise. They lie within the boundaries of the largest national park in Greece, more than 250 sq. km covering virtually all of Mikri (Small) Prespa and part of Megali (Large) Prespa in northwest Macedonia. Tall mountains, streaked with snow even in June, surround the lakes on all sides. Those to the west and north belong to Albania and FYROM, and as a sign of the changing political climate, the lakes were declared the first Balkan Park and are protected by the three countries that share them.

Serene and drowsy though it may seem now, this corner of Greece was not always at the end of the road. During the Byzantine years, long before the erection of national boundaries, Serbs and Bulgars as well as Greeks fought to build churches here and knocked down each other's castles. Under the Ottomans anchorites sought refuge in caves from Muslim and Christian roughnecks alike, and in the late 19th century, as the Ottoman Empire was crumbling, the locals were caught in a tug of war between Athens and Sofia for their sympathies and allegiance. The Greekness of Macedonia was by no means a foregone conclusion a hundred years ago. It took four years (1904-1908) of guerrilla warfare in the mountains and marshes north of Kastoria to defeat Bulgarian aspirations and Macedonia was not unified with Greece until 1913.

Up here in Macedonia there are statues of freedom fighters on every square; every village has its Pavlos Melas Street in memory of the Athenian aristocrat whose death in 1904 could be compared to Byron's in that it spurred hundreds of officers and volunteers to join the cause of their northern comrades. The area saw some action during World War II, but it was the Civil War (1946-1949) that sparked the worst devastation of all. Some of the fiercest battles between Nationalists and Communists took place near Prespes, which the guerrillas had proclaimed capital of their future socialist state. When the government forces finally won, the Communists fled behind the Iron Curtain, leaving the villages all but deserted.

Although a few survivors slowly trickled back, the government decided to repopulate the villages and revive the area by giving the land and homes of the departed *antartes* to Vlach shepherd families from other parts of Macedonia and Thessaly. Originally nomads supposedly descended from Roman legionnaires, the Vlachs speak a Latinate language but have considered themselves Greeks for centuries. It was a wise decision, given the Vlachs' reputation as hard workers.

Fifty years later, Prespes dwellers are fighting battles of a less bloody sort, but ironically the area's Greekness is again at risk. In this beautiful but isolated outpost, few young people can be persuaded to grow beans or open hotels. At least one house in three is in need of repair; many houses are beyond saving, beams and mud-and-wattle walls stand exposed, bereft of plaster.

You would think people tenacious enough to live in a remote border region would be lav-

Mountains streaked with snow even in June surround the bean farms of the Prespes

ished with incentives to remain. Instead, they're being punished. Several people told us that in the past decade the government has decided to attach some strings to their 1953 offer of land and homes. Now it is demanding that in exchange for titles and deeds never granted, the present occupants pay the State a sum equivalent to the value of the property – at current, not postwar, prices. Without owner-

ship papers no improvements can be made, no loans approved to convert to hotels, restaurants or other businesses. As one resident told me, "My parents left Yiannitsa to come here. They had to clean blood and gore off the walls and floors of the house they were given. If they'd known we'd have to pay, they would have stayed where they were." Another said, "Our children are leaving. Once there were

120 children in Agios Germanos alone; now there are only 60 in all the [12] Prespes villages combined. When I complained to the *nomarch*, all he said was, 'that's all right, there'll be more of the pie for those who stay behind'!"

But increasingly the "pie" is being made by Albanians. Like so many other places in rural Greece, they are filling the gap left by departing Greek youth. They help in the bean fields, they obtain Green Cards or citizenship and they produce much larger families. As a taverna owner said bitterly, "The government brought us here, but they don't care if the place is dying. In 10 or 20 years there'll be 80 percent Albanians and only 20 percent Greeks. The Albanians will take over."

In Psarades, the fishing village that is Greece's only settlement on Megali Prespa, everyone was depressed and tourists were few. One old man told us, "For six weeks now, we can't use our boats to take people to see the hermitages and cave paintings. They're demanding that we pay for licences, permits and life preservers. When visitors discover they can't go out in the lake, they leave."

Indeed, it was a great disappointment. The village's fleet of wooden boats was drawn up on shore, the rickety docks were empty but for a sleek white police patrol boat tied to the end of the sturdiest one. Of course, one cannot ob-

ject that such rules are being imposed; what is upsetting is that the authorities waited until the start of the 2003 tourist season to do so.

Nevertheless, even without a boat ride, the area was well worth the seven-hour drive north. We spent the first night in Psarades, wandering round its three lanes of stone houses while its flock of miniature cows – about the size of goats – ambled home, bellowing as if they were elephants. Supper was a gastronomic joy. Apart from the *gigantes* (giant beans), which were unquestionably the best we'd ever tasted, we feasted on grilled butterflied lake trout, sprinkled with hot pepper flakes; fried *tsironia* (comparable to whitebait) and, most luscious of all, a dip made from Florina red peppers, tomato purée, garlic, chilli peppers and olive oil. I made sure I got the recipe. The room above the taverna was simple but clean and I eventually fell asleep despite the chorus of a myriad frogs.

The next day, after breakfasting by the lake and purchasing a generous supply of beans, we set off on a road that is not even marked on the map. It starts from the Women's Cooperative hotel opposite Psarades. Do not miss this, especially if the boats are beached. The dirt road, pretty good except when wet, skirts the coast high above Megali Prespa with stunning views before turning inland. In early June the flowers had run riot amongst the oak, rare ju-

(above) Engine trouble?
(right) 680 metres of floating bridge
to Agios Achillios, a favoured fishing spot

niper trees and cedars, called by the locals "kedri tou Israel" not Lebanon. And I caught several glimpses of a gorgeous jay-like bird I still haven't identified, despite two good guides. Eventually we heard sheepbells and saw a long open sheepfold roofed with thatch, the hallmark of Vlach shepherds, but otherwise it seemed blissfully wild. After probably not much more than 7 km, the road joined the asphalt to Vrontero, the last village before the Albanian border, and Pyli, a hamlet on Mikri Prespa.

At Mikri Prespa, the major attraction is the islet of Agios Achillios. Once reachable only by outrageously expensive lakeboats, it is now attached to the mainland by 680 m of floating bridge. The bridge has become a favourite fishing spot, where anything from small fry to 3 kilo carp are caught with hooks baited with… kernels of canned corn! (One wonders who tried that first?) Apart from a couple of tavernas where the bridge ends, the grassy islet is deserted except for the scattered remains of five Byzantine churches nearly hidden amidst thickets of wild pear trees camouflaged by shell-pink climbing roses. The most famous is the roofless nave of Agios Achillios, built by Tsar Samuel of Bulgaria in the 10th century after his conquest of Larissa and his theft of the body of the city's patron saint. Achillios was a contemporary of Constantine the Great. In 1963 archaeologists discovered the graves of both tsar and saint, side by side and undisturbed despite a millennium of unrest.

In Prespes, a word that may derive from the Latin *praesepio* or crib, cradled as it is between mountains, there are two zones that are off-limits to visitors. One of these is the marshy area called Vromolimni at the east end of the flat strip that separates the two lakes and which is a popular nesting place for pelicans, cormorants, herons and dozens of other waders. But you can pull off the causeway here at various points to picnic, swim in Megali Prespa and birdwatch with binoculars from the shore or from special observation posts. The birds seem to congregate at either end of the strip.

Further inland is another Prespes "must", the village of Agios Germanos. This is the most attractive of the smattering of settlements inhabited mostly by bean farmers. Each of them has an imposing basilica and traditional mansions, much grander than those of Psarades. But Agios Germanos can claim the oldest church, dating back to the early 11th century, a larger number of impressive stone houses, comfortable places to stay and a good taverna.

Sadly, in the late 19th century a charmless, much larger temple to God was tacked on, like a monstrous changeling twin, to its west wall, but the early church is still a jewel and its interior covered with delicate, refined frescoes with glowing colours and a sophisticated attention to the saints' embroidered robes. (Take a torch and you will see them better.)

We could have spent more than one night in Agios Germanos – exploring the mountains above it, studying the exhibits in the Society for the Protection of Prespes Information Centre – supported by the WWF, Elliniki Etairia and the ministry of agriculture – on the village outskirts, and tracking down wildlife. One casual 15-minute stroll just off the main road turned up one large tortoise, two bright green lizards cuddling, a small spotted toad, and an extravagant purple-and-mauve orchid plus wild strawberries.

But even more satisfying were the conversations with the people we met, who were not too tired from tending their bean fields to tell us the stories that made Prespes far more fascinating than the liveliest resort. I thought about them until the nightingales sang me to sleep. ◌

The bird hospital on Agios Achillios

How to get there

The Prespes National Park is 36 km from Kastoria, 45 km from Florina. The roads are tortuous but the scenery unsurpassed.

Where to stay (area code 23850)

In Psarades, we stayed at Akrolimnia, run by Lazaros Papadopoulos (46260), which seems to have the most rooms, decorated with a certain amount of Bavarian-type kitsch. In Agios Germanos, *To Petrino* (51344) had very comfortable rooms and shower curtains (a rare find in provincial lodgings) in the bathroom. Another possibility is the *Agios Germanos* (51397), 11 rooms in a stone building with village treats for breakfast in the garden.

Where to eat

Akrolimnia in Psarades was where we had our gourmet feast. *To Tzaki* in Agios Germanos served good leek pies, homemade sausages, and chops but their giant beans could not compare with those of our first evening. There are also lakeside tavernas at Agios Achillios, Mikrolimni and Koules.

Note: A good portion of Prespes beans are organically grown and can be shipped to anywhere in Greece. The Tsikos family who own *To Petrino* will be glad to fill your order.

Agios Germanos

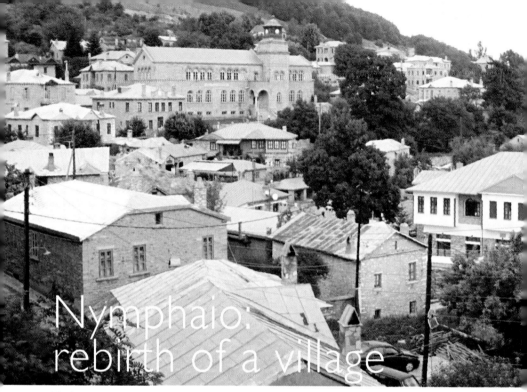

Nymphaio: rebirth of a village

The largest building in Nymphaio is a school, complete with clock tower, but it no longer has any pupils

They say that Nymphaio is the most beautiful village in northern Greece. It is certainly the most unexpected. With its elegant grey-stone houses, immaculate cobbled paths, monumental school and church, Nymphaio would not be out of place in France, Switzerland or Austria. Pink and white peonies bloom in its gardens, firs and plane trees tower over them, and no cars crowd its narrow streets. Instead there are horses, roaming free, grazing in the main square, ambling up and down the lanes – as welcomed as if they were cows in Delhi.

Five or six mares and foals greeted us as we drove into the car park at the entrance to the village, some 1,350 m above the fringes of the Thessaly plain and about 15 minutes' walk from its centre. Except for two tour buses, it was empty on that June Monday. Even the information booth was closed, but a sleepy driver told us to our immense relief that there was another car park up the hill reserved for residents and overnight guests.

At first sight, second and third, Nymphaio takes your breath away it is so handsome. As journalist Dinos Kiousis wrote in the *Kathimerini* (4/11/01), "[This is] a village that has kept its architectural tradition perfectly . . . it is delightful and spotless. Something, in other words, I haven't come across anywhere else in this country."

That Nymphaio exists at all is almost a miracle. Though it had prospered up until World War II, that war, the Civil War and the subsequent flight to the cities took their toll. By the 1980s, two-thirds of its houses were in ruins; of its prewar population of 3,500 only sixty people remained. But a few men – led by writer Nikos Mertzos and wine-maker Yiannis Boutaris – dreamed of rebuilding their birthplace and had the vision, taste and money to make it happen. They called themselves "the Last of the Mohi-

cans," and indeed they belong to a very special tribe, the Vlachs.

The word "vlachos" in Greek often has a pejorative connotation. It can mean shepherd but also "country bumpkin, clodhopper, boor." Though initially nomadic herdsmen, the Vlachs who settled in Nymphaio (and other major villages like Metsovo, Pisoderi and Kleisoura) were anything but dim-witted. They are said to be descendants of Roman Legionnaires and indeed they call themselves Armani or Aromouni, echoing the link with Rome. Of course, the Legionnaires were of mixed origins, but the Vlachs have come to be a distinct ethnic group who still speak a language with Latin roots. This has caused some scholars and a few Romanian politicians intent on land-grabbing to relate them to the Wallachians of Romania, but most Vlachs have identified themselves as one hundred percent Greek since the Revolution.

They came to Nymphaio in 1385, driven into the mountains by marauding Ottomans. At first they called it Niveasta, which has three possible etymologies, all very appropriate: Nymph, because of its stunning setting; Invisible (Ni Vista), because a high bluff shields it from view; and Snow-covered (Nives Ska), which it is much of the winter. Today almost all its glorious houses wear incongruous shiny tin roofs to encourage the snow to slide off. The early

Niveastans somehow won the protection of the Sultan's mother, Valide Sultana, who granted them the right to keep their weapons, self-government and reduced taxes. But although they settled down, they did not stay put.

The Vlachs were among the first travelling salesmen. They started by peddling animal products – milk, butter, cheese, meat, wool, fabrics – all over the Balkans. Then during their long winters, they perfected the art of designing gold and silver jewellery and in summer took their portable workshops from Constantinople to Belgrade, up the Danube and down to the Peloponnese. Before long they had opened shops in Moscow and other European cities. In the meantime, they had to use their arms as well, to defend themselves against repeated Albanian raids. They did this so effectively that, in the late 18th century, they changed the village's name to Neveska, which is said to mean something like "we're the tops".

Around the same time, those wandering shepherds turned into tobacco and cotton magnates, with factories as far afield as Egypt, Lausanne, Brussels and Oslo. One of them, the Sossidis family, became sole purveyors of cigarettes to the Turkish army, a contract so remunerative that even a hundred years later there were funds to spare for restoring their two mansions with aquamarine shutters and stone

roofs below the main square, as well as the church. But large, comfortable houses were not all these financial wizards spent their money on. Like their fellow Vlachs from Metsovo, they endowed schools, churches and public works in their homeland, while Vlach exploits in the War of Independence and struggle for Macedonia fill whole chapters in Greek history books.

Ironically, the parcelling of the Ottoman Empire into nation states stifled freedom of movement and enterprise. New borders brought customs duties, union with Greece subservience to Athens. But in 1928, the place was still flourishing. It acquired a new (Greek) name, Nymphaio, and tobacco giant Jean Nikou financed its largest building, the Nikeios School, and crowned it with a Swiss clock tower. Now Thessaloniki's Aristotelian University uses it as a conference centre.

One of the secrets to bringing Nymphaio back to life was to open hotels and restaurants that would lure city dwellers and give locals jobs. Here Yiannis Boutaris deserves a lot of the credit. He created two small pensions, La Moara and Linouria (now under new management), that in no time became famous for their cuisine as well as their understated traditional decor. Unfortunately, both are closed on Mondays, so we missed a first-hand inspection, but friends who've stayed at La Moara maintain that the staff could not be more welcoming, the food more delicious, the rooms and ambience more comfortable – well worth the expense. La Moara ranks high on every list of Greece's best small hotels.

We stayed in a converted house, the Athina built in 1900, with just five rooms decorated as they would have been when the house was new. Brass beds, embroidered curtains, art nouveau murals and lamps, faded family photographs took us back to Nymphaio a century ago, embellished by discreet mod cons. Our host, Yiannis Papadopoulos, told us of summers spent mushrooming in the woods and horseback riding on Alpine trails – "We're very fond of horses up here." He also mentioned the difficulty in building up a full time population. "The old families come back for summer vacations. It's just too hard to keep these big houses warm in winter. And there's still no school. My wife and kids live in Amyntaio during the week and come up on Friday afternoons along with the weekenders from the cities, who can't get enough of autumn leaves and snow. The village is booked up on holidays and weekends. Otherwise, it's pretty but it's empty."

That Monday night, Nymphaio's lanes were practically deserted. A few grizzled men sat in the Neveska café with a huge Pindos sheepdog; about five tourists nursed coffees in the cosy bar; and there was only one other table occupied at the Neveska restaurant – the only one open that night. But we did eat well: grilled Florina peppers, a delicately-flavoured chicken breast, and an ample carafe of the house wine, Xinomavro "tou kyriou Boutari", all for a mere 14 euros. Nymphaio water is VSOP, too, noticeably superior to the stuff we drink most of the time.

On Tuesday the museum opened, a three-storey building with a goldsmith's workshop, 19th century salon and hearth, mannequins in traditional costumes heavy with gold thread, and photos of eminent Nymphaio citizens, including one honorary one, the late president Constantine Karamanlis in Evzone kilt and clogs.

But Nymphaio is not just a pretty face aimed at evoking the past; it has a social conscience that extends beyond providing jobs to protecting wildlife. Although started by the Boutaris family, the Arcturos project has nothing to do with food and wine. From its head office in Thessaloniki, it has set up two refuges in the area – one for brown bears just outside Nymphaio in 1993, one for wolves in Agrapidia off the main road to Kastoria in 1998 – and an environmental information centre/veterinary clinic in Aetos between the two.

Both refuges exist because of man's inhumanity to animals: capturing and training bear cubs to "dance" and keeping wolves as exotic pets. Thanks to Arcturos you will never again see a dancing bear with its gypsy master in any Greek city. The last bear was brought to the refuge in 1996, raising the total to thirteen. They live on a fenced wooded slope with ponds and plenty of space (50,000 sq. m) for play and sleep, the next best thing to freedom. As refuge warden Yorgos Mostakis says, "Because of their treatment, they don't know how to behave in the wild. They wouldn't know how to bring up their young either, so we have to sterilise them."

But this is not a zoo. We have to lower our voices and peer into the shadows to catch glimpses of bears plodding between the trees or lazily wrestling. Yorgos says, "A dancing bear is not Karaghiozis [the shadow-theatre puppet hero]. We have to educate our kids to respect nature by boycotting circuses that exploit animals. But we also have to set up electric fences around places we don't want bears to go and keep our forests healthy so they don't have to raid our garbage cans for food."

We spent about an hour talking to Yorgos Mostakis, who told us the refuges are desperate for volunteers. "There are only nine people working in all three centres, two are part-time. We have had lots of volunteers from France – they don't even have to speak Greek – and we'd be grateful even for a couple of days

work. They wouldn't have to commit to a long stay, and we can offer a free room down at Aetos."

Walking back to Nymphaio – no cars are allowed within 800 m of the refuge – we heard a cuckoo chiming in the woods and spotted magenta orchids by the side of the path. Down at Aetos, however, we had the misfortune to coincide with the arrival of three school groups and experienced first hand the need for extra help. The harried woman in charge of the information centre directed us to the Wolf Refuge, but no one could be spared to show us around. There were signs of wolves inside their heavily fenced domain: paths through the underbrush, crushed bones and sheep skulls, strong smelling spoor. But the shy nocturnal animals – 17 divided into two groups in a 7 ha area – were not to be seen.

No matter. It is enough to know that an organisation like Arcturos exists and that besides looking after individual bears and wolves, it is working to preserve their habitats in Greece and in the Balkans, generally. Arcturos even managed to shift the alignment of a section of the Egnatia highway that would have encroached on a crucial wilderness area.

Nymphaio may appear empty, especially on a Monday, but there's a lot going on behind the scenes. ◯

How to get there

Nymphaio lies 610 km north of Athens, west of Veria, east of Kastoria. The most direct route from Athens is via Larissa and Kozani; from Thessaloniki drive west through Yiannitsa and Edessa.

Where to stay (area code 23860)

There are six small pensions in Nymphaio, none larger than 10 rooms. *La Moara*, 8 rooms (2310 287626), price includes breakfast and dinner; *Ta Linouria*, 10 rooms (31133); *Athina*, 5 rooms (31141). *La Betlou* (41282), *Enterne* (31230) and *La Galba* (31314) are other, slightly more economical possibilities. *La Moara* has its own stables but the other pensions can also arrange for horses and guides if you'd like to ride.

Where to eat

Besides *Neveska* and *Ta Linouria*, *La Betlou* has its own taverna, and the *Archondiko* serves traditional dishes, too. But for a special meal, try *Thomas's Taverna* at Sklithrou, in the valley west of Aetos and on the main road to Kastoria. This is no typical taverna. It's known for miles around for its cava which lists almost 300 different Greek wines, with hardly any mark up over supermarket prices. Avoid the pretentious European-sounding dishes and stick to simple Greek specialities and you won't be disappointed. Thomas is also closed on Mondays.

ARCTUROS: You can help endangered wolves and bears by visiting the refuges and buying t-shirts and other products with their logo; by adopting a bear – they eat up to 25 kg of food per day; by becoming a volunteer or by joining the society. Call 2310 554623 or check the website: www.arcturos.gr

The Macedonian
heartland: from
Vergina to Edessa

Traces of Macedonian culture are scattered between Naoussa and Edessa: four temple-like tombs with frescoes almost as bright as the day they were painted and Aristotle's Peripatetic School. This was the Harvard of ancient Greece.

We hadn't ventured north since the summer of 1981 when the dog died. Sobbing, we'd dug a grave under the fig tree in the back yard, thrown a few essentials into the back of the car and driven non-stop to Thessaloniki. The Vergina finds had just been put on display in the museum there; we hoped they'd dry our tears, and they did.

In those days, the site of the Macedonian tombs was closed to the public because the excavations were still in progress. They finally opened, in November 1997, and a few months later we set off for Vergina, clear eyed this time. It was an ordinary March weekend, so the dozens of buses from places as far afield as Gytheion, Patras and Nea Smyrni came as a nasty surprise. Children of all sizes shrieked, clamoured and whined in front of the entrance

as thick as bees round a hive. The queue – or that shapeless mass that passes for one in this country – was at least eight people wide and goodness knows how many hundreds long, so we retreated outside the gates to rethink. (*Identical throngs greeted us at the end of May 2005, so plan your trip for a winter weekday, if possible.*)

The village of Vergina did not exist until refugees from Asia Minor settled there in 1923 so it boasts nothing to hold one's attention. But the royal palace of the Macedonian kings overlooks it from a wooded hill, so up we went. To be precise, nothing remains of the palace except the foundations and a sense of spacious majesty that comes from its lofty setting above the great plain. A long ramp-like path leads up to it, flanked by lichen-dappled column segments that made me think of an honour guard. As we stared at the covered mosaic floor, willing the sand to be blown away – even a small patch would do – a flock of shaggy goats jangled by, reminding us that this was Aigai. A Roman historian wrote that Karanos, the mythical founder of the Macedonian dynasty, followed a herd of goats (*aiges*) to this site, which would become the capital of the kingdom until Philip's grandfather Archelaos moved it to Pella. And it was in the theatre below the palace that Philip II was assassinated in 336 BC and, as we all know now, laid to rest in the cemetery in the plain. Tradition ruled that every Macedonian king would have to be buried there or the line would disintegrate, a prophecy fulfilled instantly by the chaos that reigned after Alexander's burial in Egypt.

Travellers and earlier archaeologists had long known about the palace and the tumulus below it but that same Roman historian had said that Aigai was situated at or near Edessa. As a consequence, nobody, not even Manolis Andronikos who eventually excavated it, suspected that the enormous Hellenistic cemetery at Vergina was also the legendary royal one. Today, only a few disgruntled residents of Edessa, smarting at their loss of glory, stubbornly dispute the evidence.

By two o'clock, the hordes had largely dispersed so we returned to the enclosure and

The gold coffin holding King Phillip II's remains is among Aigai's many treasures

filed down the sloping corridor into what must be Greece's most impressively reconstructed archaeological site. One descends underground, as if penetrating the giant tumulus, where three tombs stand intact, together with cases containing the most spectacular of the finds (the rest are still in Thessaloniki) and excellent descriptions in Greek and flawless English. This beautiful piece of staging allows one to experience a

The waterwheel was part of a hemp factory in the good old days

bit of the tremendous excitement of Andronikos and his team as they slowly began to realise what they had unearthed – four tombs (one was destroyed) and the most important one unplundered. We stood speechless before the Rape of Persephone painted on the walls of the otherwise empty first tomb by an artist as brilliant as any Renaissance master. Whoever rendered Pluto's grimace of lust and victory as

he draws the lovely girl into his hurtling chariot, their swirling robes or her mother's despair as she sits shrouded on the mirthless stone must have been the Leonardo of his day. (*The original is no longer on display and one must be content with a reproduction rendered outside the tomb.*)

I tore myself away to continue the route to the other tombs and finds: Philip's tomb with its hunting frieze containing royal portraits, the famous gold larnaces with the sixteen-pointed Macedonian star, the delicate gold wreaths, the reconstituted funerary couches with their miniature ivory portrait heads of Philip, Alexander and Alexander's mother, the purple and gold cloth in which the queen's bones were wrapped, the asymmetrical greaves for the lame king's shins, his gold-trimmed suit of armour, and even the ashes from the funeral pyre through which golden rosettes and acorns still glint. After an hour or so I finally emerged into the sunlight, blinking with the brightness but also with emotion at the words written by Andronikos just after he'd made the discovery of his life and now inscribed near the exit:

"And then we saw a sight which it was not possible for me to have imagined, because until then such an ossuary had never been found; an all-gold lamax with an impressive relief star on its lid. We lifted it from the sarcophagus, placed it on the floor and opened it. Our eyes nearly popped out of their sockets and our breathing stopped; there, unmistakably, were charred bones placed in a carefully formed pile and still retaining the colour of the purple cloth in which they had once been wrapped… We felt the need to return to the light and to take deep gulps of fresh air. When I was once more outside I moved a little apart from my colleagues on the excavation, the visitors and the police and stood alone to recover from that unbelievable sight. Everything indicated that we had found a royal tomb; and if the dating we had assigned to the objects was correct, as it seemed to be, then… I did not even dare to think about it. For the first time a shiver ran down my spine, something akin to an electric shock passed through me. If the dating… and if these were the royal remains… then… had I held the bones of Philip in my hands? It was far too terrifying an idea for my brain to assimilate."

Andronikos died in 1992 but he gave the Greeks and anyone who visits this extraordinary museum some thrilling pieces to a puzzle that lies at the core of European history.

After this insight into the past, a tour of the modern towns of Veria, Naoussa and Edessa was bound to be an anticlimax. Somehow I had expected this area of orchards and vines to resemble Pelion, the villages to be perfectly preserved examples of Macedonian half-timbering and slate roofs. Well, I was wrong.

But orchards there are aplenty. Miles and miles of peach and apricot trees, meticulously pruned, tinted the entire plain a deep pink as far as the eye could sea. Pink blossoms so thick, so dense, so overwhelming they rewrote Andrew Marvell: "annihilating all that's made to a pink thought in a pink shade."

Edessa and Naoussa produce some of Greece's most glorious fruit – apricots, peaches and cherries

The towns themselves all occupy a steep escarpment that rises straight out of the plain. Not until you're actually in the old centres are any traditional vestiges apparent among the tall apartment blocks that Osbert Lancaster once compared to dressers with open drawers. But Veria and Edessa have been settled continuously since the 5th century BC or thereabouts so little nuggets of interest can be ferreted out. The Roman general Pompey encamped in Veria one winter and St. Paul preached there. At the top of the town, Veria's history is synopsised in the cluster of buildings around the clockless Plateia Orologiou: the acropolis on which a crumbling Byzantine tower squats, the synagogue (now bereft of its parishioners), a mosque, a newly restored 19th century high school and the so-called bema from which St. Paul delivered his sermons. Scattered among the pedestrianised streets below the square are a charming Ottoman baths complex, a patch of Roman road, a collection of typical Macedonian houses converted into tavernas and nightclubs, plus anywhere from 40 to 60 old churches, depending on which guidebook you open. Sadly, although whole books have been published on the paintings they conceal, most of the churches are firmly locked.

But while Veria was a pleasant place to poke round, Naoussa was a complete disappointment. Heralded by flamboyant acrylic blankets draped along the side of the road, the former "Manchester of the Balkans" appeared to be a collection of derelict factories, leftover Carnival pennants and post-War cement with only one imposing slate-roofed, half-timbered church.

Edessa's soothing streams and tree-canopied streets made a better impression. Of course, anyone expecting Niagara Falls will not be bowled over by Edessa's cataracts, but the water whooshing, rippling and tumbling alongside the pavements and under little bridges creates a holiday atmosphere. We meandered around the pools and terraces shaded by mighty plane trees and wound up the evening in Merakles' ouzeri, feasting on Macedonian treats like red pepper puree (the hotter the better), grilled pancetta (a bit like spare ribs), pungent "batsos" cheese, chili pepper pickle and a wonderful local red wine. "Tomorrow," said the owner's brother, "have a look round the cathedral. It's built on ancient foundations. They belonged to the palace where Alexander was born. The one near Veria? That was just a country house."

Naoussa and Edessa, 2005

Returning to Naoussa seven years later, I found the town still a muddle. Far fewer blankets flapped on the roadside. The loss of virtually all its textile operations to Turkey has sent many jobless people trudging to Skopje for work. Not all Balkan migration is southward.

It did not help that we got caught in a series of May downpours, which made it impractical to visit the town's reputedly attractive parks or to discover which modern districts were concealing the pretty old buildings in the tourist brochures. We did learn by chance though that there were no brothels nor bouzoukia anywhere in Naoussa. City fathers long ago prohibited such forms of entertainment as a sign of perpetual mourning for the horrific butchery committed by Turks here in 1822. As at Zalongo in Epirus, mothers and children leapt off a cliff, in this case into a waterfall, to escape a worse fate.

But if the city's charms remain elusive, those of its surroundings positively burst out. Most conspicuous are the vineyards. Spread out in all

The Peripatetic School isn't much to look at, but this is where Aristotle taught his most illustrious pupil, Alexander

directions, their serried rows cover every plateau, field and hillside with bibulous promise. One of the country's foremost red-wine-producing regions, Naoussa has been making tipplers happy since the middle of the 19th century. At Boutari & Sons stuccoed mustard premises at Stenimachos (23320 41666), we saw labels printed in Salonica in the 1880s bearing three languages – French, Arabic (Osmanli) and Hebrew. Another vinter, Yiannis Dalamara (23320 26054) on the main road up to Naoussa, showed us the deed to his great-great grandfather's first vineyard in 1840 while we tasted a nice light *xinomavro* blend in the family's original distillery, now a small museum. At least twelve other vineyards in the area welcome visitors, including Kyr Yiannis (another Boutari).

Less obvious are the traces of Macedonian

Ripe cherries, one of the rewards for sightseeing in late spring

were the backdrop to Aristotle's lessons to his most illustrious pupil, Alexander, and that makes it special indeed.

In contrast to Naoussa, Edessa's old district, Varosi, has received several facelifts since 1998. Many delightful buildings have been painstakingly restored, two into atmospheric hotels run by young locals. In the green main park, weeping willows, the hemp factory/aquarium/open air museum and all that water coursing through it spin more magic than before – when the tour buses have left. Not for nothing was Edessa called Vodena, Slavic for "lots of water".

Instead of peach blossoms, we found ripe cherries this time and they brought out the glutton in me. My lips were purple by the time we'd driven to the Loutraki spa near Aridea about 30 km to the north, not far from the FYROM border and the ski slope on Mt. Kaimaktsalan.

Alas we had fallen on another school outing day. Flocks of excited, unruly children filled the pool, their shouts echoing through the woods, bouncing off the waterfalls. A couple of oblivious elders soaked in a basin under a small cataract.

I envied them but went in search of more cherries instead.

The moral of this story? The heart of Macedonia is too beautiful and fascinating to have all to yourself. ◎

culture scattered between Naoussa and Edessa: four temple-like tombs with frescoes almost as bright as the day they were painted and Aristotle's Peripatetic School. This was the Harvard of ancient Greece, but since it never boasted ivy-covered halls in the first place, there's not much to see. Above a boggy pond where nymphs frolicked stands a flat terrace, carved out of the hillside. But its two small caves, niches and steps

How to get there

If you don't have a car and happen to be in Thessaloniki, consider taking the train to Edessa. It must be the cheapest train ride in Greece, 3 euros for the one hour journey. It will land you at the old station and the Stathmos restaurant next door, one of the best in northern Greece.

Where to stay

In Edessa, two charming choices in the old district are *Varosi* (23810 21865, www.varosi.gr), and *Hagiati* (23810 51500, www.hagiati.gr). Both are restored family houses run by delightful people with taste.

At Loutraki, *Pozar Pension* (23840 91159), cheap and peaceful, comes highly recommended by friends.

In or rather just outside Naoussa, comfortable *Esperides* (23320 20250, www.esperideshotel.gr) on the main road into town is well placed for visits to Vergina, the vineyards and the Macedonian tombs.

Where to eat

O Stathmos, under the trees in summer, next to the fireplace in winter, is worth the trip north. We dined superbly on piglet casserole, courgette fritters, a copious salad and the best grilled mushrooms we've ever tasted, local wine (of course) with fresh fruit and oriental pastries on the house, for 26 euros! It's open for lunch and dinner. Outside Naoussa, you can buy and taste traditional sweets, pickles and pastas at *Syntagi tis Yiayias*.

The Varosi in Edessa

The allure
of Thessaloniki

Ironically, the city's symbol, the White Tower (opposite), was built not by Greeks but by Suleiman the Magnificent. Under the Turks, it was a prison and the Janissaries executed so many prisoners there that it earned the name Bloody Tower.

It could be a case of the grass being greener, or the sea being closer, but whenever I go to Thessaloniki, I want to move there. The constant presence of the water, the sight of Olympos's snowy peaks floating above the horizon never fail to captivate. And then again, it looks so much more like a real city than Athens. In the tradition of Central Europe, it has broad avenues and open squares, whereas Athens is more the East, dense and mostly unplanned. Despite two disastrous earthquakes and the even more devastating fire of 1917, despite an unhealthy percentage of anonymous apartment blocks and even fewer parks than the Athenian megalopolis, Thessaloniki seems grander, with a capital's air of self-assurance. Many more dowager buildings from the 19th and 20th century – buildings with art deco

A resplendent Alexander the Great rides on horseback but it was his half-sister after whom Thessaloniki was named

façades, neoclassical elements or fanciful peaked towers – have escaped the wreckers' ball. Factories, customs houses and red-light districts have been transformed into party places and exhibition areas, and the city keeps acquiring new architectural masterpieces, like the Megaro Mousikis, the Museum of Contemporary Art or the Bissell Library. Meanwhile, the more distant past keeps popping up wherever you go.

Admittedly, it has no Parthenon presiding over us modern midgets from a lofty Acropolis. None of Thessaloniki's monuments is quite so evocative on its own. But what you do have is a sense of continuity, of history as being a linear succession of conquerors, all of whom have left a presence – reminders of war and brutality but also of faith in God and in commerce. Since its founding in 315 BC by King Kassander of Macedonia, who named it after his wife, Alexander the Great's half-sister, Thessaloniki has always been the most important city between Constantinople and Rome. It was little more than a century and a half old when the Romans took it over, building the Via Egnatia to link Asia with Italy. Not surprisingly vestiges of Roman rule outnumber Hellenistic – the forum, a triumphal arch, a very ruined imperial palace and the Rotunda. Agios Georgios, as it is now called, itself encapsulates well over a thousand years of the city's history. Originally intended as the mausoleum of the co-emperor Galerius, it afterwards became a church and then a mosque; the only minaret in town rises next to it.

Byzantine Thessaloniki runs throughout the city, sometimes, surprisingly, at a metre or so below street level. Its churches large and small are far more numerous and impressive than Athens' humble miniatures; long stretches of crenellated walls still cordon off some of the older districts; while several museums have fine collections of mosaics, icons and ecclesiastical lore.

Ironically, the city's symbol, the White Tower, was built not by Greeks but by Suleiman the Magnificent. Under the Turks, it was a prison and the Janissaries executed so many prisoners there that it earned the name Bloody Tower. A little whitewash after the Ottoman reforms in the 1870s did wonders for its image. Now it is a museum of the city's history.

Apart from the Eptapyrgio or Yedi Koulé near the walls, a fortress with seven towers that until recently also served as a prison, most of Ottoman Thessaloniki shows itself in peaceful relics – the graceful brick hammams or public baths, mosques and closed bazaars scattered through the centre of town. Not as tall or as imposing as the churches, their domed roofs resemble inverted soup plates like the helmets worn by British soldiers in World War I. Some of the baths were operating as late as 1968. Now they may be flower markets, cinemas or museums.

Perhaps less conspicuous than the Roman, Byzantine or Turkish heritage, but certainly more pervasive is the imprint left by Thessaloniki's Jewish community. At the end of the 19th

The stately and ageless Aristotelous Square is a prime meeting spot,
like Syntagma with a little Paris thrown in

century, with a population of 70,000, Jews out-numbered both Muslims and Christians put to-gether. Their conquest occurred without weapons or threats as Sephardim from Spain and then Portugal accepted the Sultan's offer of sanctuary from Catholic monarchs ordering them to convert or move out. It must be said that the Sultan was no bleeding heart; he saw the Jews as a solution to the repopulation and revival of Thessaloniki, which was still semi-deserted and in ruins after the massacres and

looting inflicted by his armies in 1430, sixty years before.

They were by no means the first. Jews had been living in Thessaloniki as early as the 1st century BC, and possibly earlier. These Romaniote Jews were Hellenised and Greek-speaking. As persecutions escalated in the 14th and 15th century, Ashkenazim arrived from Hungary and Germany, while other Sephardim trickled in from Sicily and the Italian mainland, some of which was under Spanish rule. By 1515 Jewish tailors and textile merchants were outfitting the entire Ottoman army. By 1537 Thessaloniki or Salonica had a new epithet, "Mother of Israel".

But where the Jews made the most impact was on the city of the late 19th-early 20th century. Controlling well over half of its businesses, they erected the Allatini flour mill, banks, the customs house and the main market, as well as hospitals, orphanages, schools and an old age home. Many of the villas still standing on Vassilissis Olgas Avenue – also known as the Boulevard of Chateaux – were their family residences. More ostentatious than discreet, they broadcast their owners' wealth and position, all the more poignant since practically none of their descendants survived the Holocaust.

Although for decades commemorating the Jewish presence was a perennial subject for discussion rather than action, by the end of the 20th century Thessaloniki had acquired a long-overdue Holocaust memorial. And in 2002 the community finally got the museum it deserves. The new Jewish Museum "honors the rich and creative Sephardic heritage as it evolved in the city after the 15th century." Curated by Nicholas Hannan Stavroulakis, who also set up and was the first director of the Jewish Museum in Athens, it occupies a building that once housed a major bank and a Jewish newspaper.

With a glass roof, black and white marble floors and bright white walls, there is nothing morose about it. But what saddened me was the dearth of material; so much was destroyed in the 1917 fire, when 53,737 Jews were left homeless, and by the Nazis, who even bulldozed their cemetery. Nevertheless, placard-sized period photographs, postcards and date charts bring the history to life, while imaginatively displayed Torah scrolls, costumes and mementos of happy social occasions reveal deeply held traditions and normalcy. The final room, dedicated to the last chapter in the story, still comes as a shock. Standing in the middle is the machine that cut out the yellow stars of David all Jews were forced to wear. The story ends abruptly in March 1943 with the shipping of some 49,000 persons to Auschwitz and Bergen-Belsen. Only 4 percent returned. Today there are about 1,200 Jews living in Thessaloniki.

One of the most enduring legacies of the Jewish community is the market built in 1922 by Eli Modiano in the heart of town. Covering a whole city block, it pulses with energy day and night. Though jammed with stalls selling every kind of edible commodity – raw or cooked, loose or packaged – it is not quite as loud and chaotic as its counterpart on Athinas Street. And because so many of its goods reflect the culinary traditions of Asia Minor and the Balkans, it seems even more exotic. There are bar-

You're never far from the sea on Thessaloniki

rels of whole cabbages soaking in brine, laven-der aubergines wrapped around fire-engine-red Florina peppers, unctuous olive paste gleaming in tubs, salted fish in every imaginable manifes-tation, feta from all over Greece, including (would you believe!) Fet Lait, sides of scarlet pastourma reeking of paprika and garlic, bread boutiques, and even a dainty little corner with green and yellow liqueurs made from herbs and prettily wrapped spices.

By night, the block next to the Modiano market, also full of small shops, turns into a wall-to-wall taverna. A stylish green metal/glass-panelled frame roofs the alleyways and tables,

keeping diners dry and warm in all weather. Only as old as this century, it is a good example of how well Thessaloniki utilises its landmarks. This used to be the Jewish quarter of Poulia, settled by immigrants from Southern Italy.

Another example of a neighbourhood given more than just a facelift is Ladadika, closer to the port. I suppose it could be compared to the Athenian Psyrri, since both are former red-light districts. Besides bordellos, the Ladadika was a rough area of warehouses, where stevedores took oil, olives and dry goods off the ships for storage. It was the only slice of commercial Thessaloniki to survive the Great Fire. Now it is mostly bars and restaurants, some of them excellent. A bit like a stage set, it could be criticised as too gentrified. Nevertheless, it's an extremely pleasant place to meet.

The prime meeting spot is Aristotelous Square, Thessaloniki's Syntagma. Although it dates from after the fire, it has a stately ageless quality. Open to the sea on the south, its northern buildings rest on arcades and close off the wide expanse with gentle curves. It was designed by the French architect Hébrard in sweeping Parisian accents, and other buildings in the vicinity are equally eye-catching. This is a good place to people watch, as sooner or later everyone – Balkan businessmen or local yuppies, Ukrainian shopgirls or mothers with toddlers – turns up here to sit in its chic cafés or simply amble. Unlike Syntagma it is blissfully free of automobiles.

The same cannot be said for other parts of the city, which make Athenian traffic look streamlined, but so many exciting eateries, shops and sights are within walking distance, you rarely need a car. An exception is the nightspot area west of town, where Mylos and VILKA pull in crowds every evening. Once a flour mill and a textile factory, these are one-stop entertainment complexes, with theatres, cinemas, art galleries, shops, bars and restaurants, as attractively converted as Athens' old Gas Works but considerably livelier.

On my most recent pilgrimage to Greece's second city, I made a point of visiting two splendid and very different museums. Both the Macedonian Museum of Contemporary Art and the Museum of Byzantine Culture are modern architectural masterpieces, while the latter had just been awarded Museum of the year 2005 by the Council of Europe, but I was unprepared for the beauty and drama of their spaces. In the first, an airy three-storey spiral shows off works by Niki de Saint-Phalle, Takis and other modernists once owned by Alexander Iolas, with temporary exhibitions arranged in bright halls to the left. In the second, attractive brick walls outside and in form the backdrop for a concise pageant of Christian art and civilisation in Thessaloniki from the 4th to the 19th century. This is no collection of stiff saints and sombre Virgins. Instead, columns, reliefs, mosaics and ingenious blown-up photographs whisk you into the enthralling atmosphere of an early basilica. From there, ten more galleries, seamlessly attached by a gentle ramp, lead you through houses, burial grounds, the abrupt change imposed by the Iconoclasts, castles, and a declining Byzantium, all made vivid by exemplary lighting and explanatory texts.

Bravo Thessaloniki. I wonder what next year's visit will reward us with. ⭘

How to get there

There are several flights per day between Athens and Thessaloniki. Or you can take the Intercity train (OSE, 210 5297777), which is modern and streamlined and stops at fewer stations along the way than the regular service. And, there's always the Intercity Bus (KTEL, 210 8225148) or your own car. Count on the drive taking at least 5 hours, depending on the traffic.

Where to stay (area code 2310)

There are hotels for every pocket-book, from the ultra luxurious *Hyatt Regency* near the airport to youth hostels. Try to find something central, near Aristotelous Square, which is within walking distance of most of the major sights. *Le* (sic) *Palace* (Tsimiski 12 (257400) is a good, reasonably priced option.

Note: The Jewish Museum, 13 Ag. Mina Street (250406/7), is open from 11 am-2 pm, every day except Saturday. On Wednesday and Thursday it is also open from 5-8 pm. The Museum of Byzantine Culture, 2 Leoforos Stratos, is open daily. Call 868570 for exact times. The Macedonian Museum of Contemporary Art, just a block away from the Byzantine Museum, lies within the international fair grounds. Few Salonicans know of its existence but it is worth a visit just to see the Alexander Iolas collection (282567).

Where to eat

Thessaloniki is a food lover's paradise, where you can find everything from haute French, Mexican and Chinese to the whole range of Greek eateries. Don't leave without going to a fish place – the city's mussel dishes are renowned; *Archipelagos* (435800) and *Hamodrakas* (447943), both in Nea Krini, are two of the best. My favourite ouzeri/ restaurant is *Aristotelous*, in an arcade just up from the square, number 8 on the street of the same name. It serves dozens of *mezedes* in a courtyard filled with flowers, potted plants and an old world atmosphere. Local friends love *Zythos* in Ladadika and *Dore Zythos*, opposite the White Tower, and the tavernas around the Modiano market are always jammed, which must mean something. The *Terkenlis* pastry shop at Tsimiskis and Aristotelous, in business since 1948, always has me drooling. There is not a thing in the window that isn't both stunning and mouth-watering, and I never leave the city without succumbing to a three-tiered cone of homemade ice cream.

Off the beaten track in Halkidiki

Mosaic swirl at Amphipolis

> While a drive on Kassandra's ring road reveals that construction has by no means stopped, almost any minor lane down to the beach or into the hills leaves the cement out of sight and out of mind.

'd forgotten Halkidiki was so beautiful. I'd resisted going back there for the past twenty something years because I feared it had turned into one huge resort. Now that I finally succumbed I wonder that the region isn't even more developed. Thick forests cover most of this curiously shaped three-legged peninsula, which looks like a scraggly, smaller version of the Peloponnese pasted onto the middle of Macedonia. Startlingly white beaches hem all its coasts and the sea lapping them contains every shade of blue in the spectrum, from the palest turquoise to the deepest sapphire.

Not surprisingly, a good many of these idyllic beaches have attracted hotels, bungalows, maisonettes, villas and "rooms" in such profusion that their appeal has vanished for this loner. But as we roamed, up and down Kassandra and Sithonia, to the very borders of Mt. Athos and up the slopes of Mt. Holomontas, we discovered that Halkidiki has a welter of unbeaten tracks far too narrow for the tourist bus.

Even on Kassandra. The first of the prongs on what a poet might compare to Poseidon's trident, Kassandra is to Thessalonikans what the Sounion coast is to Athenians. It's their play-

assandra's oval quasi lake, Glarokavos,
pens to the sea at just one spot

Maybe this was the view from Aristotle's house in Stageira

ground, where they flock on weekends and holidays (though they choose more distant destinations for longer vacations), for swinging nightclubs and glamourous pool-bars. Thus it was the first to be exploited and remains the most crowded. But while a drive on Kassandra's ring road reveals that construction has by no means stopped, almost any minor lane down to the beach or into the hills leaves the cement out of sight and out of mind.

At Polychrono, a little arrow pointing to "turtles" sent us swerving up a dirt road until muddy ruts forced us out of the car. We walked for half an hour amongst meadows and forests, streams and birdsong, without even spotting a tortoise. The next day a friend who leads treks told us that another two hours of climbing would have brought us to the turtle pond, an unexpected dimple in the mountain ridge that bisects Kassandra.*

A few kilometres later, we followed a dusty track that led to the oval quasi-lake of Glarokavos. It is open to the sea at just one spot, where water funnels between whiter than white sand dunes rimmed with luxuriant pine trees. Small boats parked in the protected waters, a straw-hatted woman was fishing with five rods; there was not a hotel in sight.

Usually we avoided the towns. Even before Kassandra and Sithonia began attracting tourists, most of the coastal settlements were not marvels of traditional architecture. In addition to the purely touristic villages that are no more than a decade or two old, there are many others that did not exist before 1922. In that devastating year when some three millennia of the Greek presence in Asia Minor came to a cruel and abrupt end, thousands of refugees poured into the country, particularly Macedonia and Thrace, seeking homes and jobs. Up until then much of southern Halkidiki had been the preserve of the great monasteries of Mount Athos, the third prong of the trident. But with the emergency, they donated an enormous percentage of their estates, known as *metochia*, to the refugee cause. Villages sprouted, some like Nea Fokea

and Neos Marmaras named after lost homelands. Since the '70s, though, expansion has been so rapid that it has engulfed the original core hamlets or transformed them beyond recognition.

One exception to this rule is Afytos. Situated one-third of the way down Kassandra's east coast, it is perhaps the only town in Halkidiki that has held the same location and the same name since antiquity (when it was Aphytis). Until now. The authorities are rechristening it to Athytos. "You see," said a local, "it doesn't seem right that such a lush area should be called 'plantless'." Athytos retains the sound without the meaning.

Besides being full of trees and flowers, the old centre can be proud of its carless cobbled streets, Macedonian style houses in mint condition with intimate courtyards, thick stone walls and wooden *hayiatia* (overhanging upper floors), and beguiling shops whose hand-painted signs outnumber plastic and neon. But this is not all. The town comes to a sudden halt at the edge of a cliff, whose every inch is occupied by a café or taverna with a superb view up the coast, across to Sithonia and down to the beaches at its foot. One more boon: because it faces east, there is no competition as to which can claim the best sunset.

Besides having few buildings that are more than a century old, Halkidiki also lacks impressive ancient ruins. This is not because it had no past. Instead, its past was rather too full of drama. If you discount the Petralona cave where the peninsula's first residents lived between 75,000 and 50,000 years ago and scattered Bronze Age remains, its recorded history began around the 7th century BC when adventurers from Euboea (today's Evia) founded some thirty colonies round its shores. Although a few were from Eretria, Chalkis (today's Halkida) spawned the lion's share and gave the region its name.

The Euboeans intermarried with the local tribes but over the next centuries their cities became embroiled in the Persian invasions, the deadly Athens vs Sparta squabble and Philip II's Macedonian supremacy campaign. They were destroyed, abandoned and/or rebuilt time and again, and this pattern continued into the Christian era as pirates and then Ottomans vied with Byzantines. Finally, earthquakes and quarrying of old acropolises and forts for building materials have left little more than the occasional watchtower, crumbling wall and basilica foundation.

One wonderful exception to this rule (Halkidiki is full of exceptions) is Stageira, a naturally fortified promontory way over on the east coast of Halkidiki north of Mount Athos. This was where Aristotle was born in 384 BC, and although it merits but half a line in my *Blue Guide*, I discovered its high walls enclosed all

sorts of interesting piles of stone connected by shrub lined paths. Besides the usual shrines and stoas, there was the very identifiable layout of a Hellenistic house. Of course, it hadn't belonged to Aristotle, but the idea thrilled me that I might be standing in his footsteps, captivated by the same view.

It's even possible that he enjoyed the same treat for lunch. Below the ancient site, Olympiada, named for Alexander the Great's mother, is famous for having the fattest mussels in northern Greece. They are at least twice the size and twice as sweet as any I've tasted anywhere. Olympiada is an anomaly – a little fishing port with a pretty beach that is neither tacky nor swanky. It seems to exist in a time warp, a reminder of the days before packaged tourism changed the face of seaside settlements.

Olympiada has escaped resort fever because it is sitting too close to a gold mine. Mining is nothing new to this corner of Halkidiki, which is riddled with shafts and tunnels dug by Greeks, Romans, Byzantines and Ottomans to extract silver, lead, iron and, by the 16th century, gold. But the most recent efforts demarcated the area as industrial, keeping tourism at bay. Despite the promise of riches far greater from the Canadian company, TVX Gold, local unrest forced TVX to pull out in 2003 after seven years of erratic activity. Fears of water pollution

Ouranoupoli, as close to the holy mountain as half of us will ever get

was the reason we heard most often, but the issue remains murky.

Mining seemed remote on the lush mountains of Stratoniko and Holomontas, where the only gold sprang from exuberant bursts of jasmine-scented broom that at times made the forest more yellow than green. A gorgeous road dipped and soared like an extended roller coaster straight through the woods, at times branching off to a sleepy village. And yet, this was the district of the *mademohoria* – villages that traditionally lived from the mines (*madem* in Turkish). In the days of the empire, they flourished, blessed with privileges and a percentage of the profits.

We stopped in one of the largest of them, Arnea, a place I'd never heard of before. A charming collection of attractive Macedonian houses around a large stone church and bell-tower, it looked like the honey capital of Greece rather than a mining town. Amber jars of the gooey stuff filled the windows of every shop on the main square. Its women used to weave but the handicraft organisation's shelves were virtually bare and the Folk Art Museum was shut, as is so often the case in rural areas. So I turned to my guidebook for some clues to Arnea's history. Apparently, the Turks burnt it to the ground in 1821 and in 1928 its name was changed from Liaringovi – a completely understandable adjustment when you think that this Slavic word is said to have meant "pile of manure".

After the catastrophe of '21, Arnea must have bounced back. One hotel, the Alexandrou Inn, has been lovingly restored and decorated in the manner of the late 19th century. Antimacassars and brass bedsteads, Victorian chairs and old photos portray a comfortable bourgeois way of life. "It was our dream to reopen it as an inn," said Takis Alexandrou, who owns it with his brother, Vassilis. "My grandfather ran it as a *hani*, with stables on the ground floor and rooms upstairs. I love the continuity."

Continuity was certainly lacking in Oura-noupoli, the gateway to the Holy Mountain. Back in the late 70s when I waited there while my man trekked to the legendary monasteries, it was an unmemorable conglomeration of rooms, small hotels and tavernas huddled around the austere, almost windowless Prosphorion tower. Now an irreverent billboard for the Wet Dreams Beach Bar heralds the new "Heaven City": mammoth luxury hotels, luna parks with elaborate waterslides, a crush of eateries, and souvenir shops offering guides to Mount Athos in at least a dozen different languages, including Japanese and various Cyrillic tongues. Only the tower, a relic from the 14th or 12th century depending on your source, stands unviolated above a strand of immaculate white beach.

But even here, there lurked another exception to the rule of rampant development. Maybe more. The first is a small hotel called Skites, named after the cells ascetics retreat to in twos and threes. Located a short kilometre from the border with Mount Athos, where signs threaten severe punishment for female trespassers, this delightful refuge is worlds away from the hubbub of Ouranoupoli. With its airy rooms, bountiful gardens and a terrace overlooking the sea where concerts are held on summer evenings, it would be a wonderful base for further exploration. Not only could you take

the usual cruise around Mount Athos, the island of Ammouliani is just a 15-minute ferry ride from nearby Trypiti. So-called because of its wealth of beaches (*ammos* meaning sand), Ammouliani is the largest of a string of offshore islets. From the mainland, they looked completely unspoiled.

I longed to go but Sithonia beckoned. The middle prong of Poseidon's trident is higher, greener and less built up than Kassandra (leaving aside the immense complex at Porto Carras on its west coast which has almost two thousand beds). Scooting down the east side, we passed one electrifying view after another. My guidebook described the beaches below as "idyllic", "romantic", "tropical" etc. Tempted, we'd spin off the main road only to find that the beach in question had been commandeered by a humongous camping ground or that it was cordoned off by a caterpillar chain of mobile homes that had already staked their claim.

Nevertheless, we persevered until we found an unblemished sliver of paradise. By now we had learned that in Halkidiki there is an exception to every rule. ○

* Although this area was destroyed by fire in 2006, there is another turtle pond near the Sani wetlands. Kassandra's forests are still intact to the west and south.

How to get there

One way would be to fly to Thessaloniki and rent a car if you can't face the long drive. But a car really is essential for exploring both the legs and the mountains of this diverse region.

Where to stay

In Kassandra, *Petrino Suites* (2374 091635 or -39) just before Afytos on the main road south may not be on the beach but it makes up for that in many ways. It has 30 duplex apartments arranged in flower-bedecked stone cottages at various distances from a large swimming pool. It also boasts a wonderful taverna, with tables by the fire in winter and under shady poplar trees in summer.

In Ouranoupoli, *Skites* is as close as females will ever get to the Holy Mountain and so lovely you won't even mind missing it. (23770 71140, info@skites.gr and www.skites.gr). If it's full, try the *Xenia*, nicely renovated and not far from the heart of town (23770 71412).

In Arnea, *Alexandrou Inn* (23720 23210-1), is a typical Macedonian family house restored and converted by two architects who spend most of their time restoring monasteries on Mount Athos. Staying here will take you back to the late 19th century but with all mod cons. Spiros Litsis, the Northern Epirot caretaker, and his wife will make you feel welcome. They are both marvellous cooks.

Where to eat

Petrino, *Skites* and *Alexandrou Inn* all have their own, exceptional restaurants. Otherwise, we found the fattest mussels that ever plopped into our greedy mouths at Olympiada, under the ruins of Stageira, in a quintessential Greek taverna whimsically called *To Germaniko*.

Annea's colourful old houses

eastern
Macedonia
and Thrace

Lake Kerkini:
a delicate balance

The sound of drums wafted in and out of our siesta.
The *Anastenarides* or Fire Walkers were beginning
the rituals leading up to their famous dance on hot coals
on the night of May 21st.

A t nine-thirty on this May morning Lake Kerkini is smooth as polished pewter and almost the same colour. The mountains to the north and south are darker shadows in the mist, while on the eastern horizon a long row of trees looks like a hem of raggedy grey velvet separating sea and sky. Fish plop with an eccentric rhythm as if playing a John Cage composition, sleek cormorants and grebes with blond crests disappear under the metallic surface, and several Dalmatian pelicans float serenely by, causing barely a ripple. There are so many here, it doesn't seem possible that they're in danger of becoming extinct. At intervals along the shore, blue herons stand like sentinels among the grasses, beige squacco herons a third their size perch in the branches of dead trees. A night heron,

black as its name, streaks across the water in front of our *plava*, the narrow, flat-bottomed boat typical of Macedonia's lakes.

Among Greece's eleven protected wetlands, Lake Kerkini, north of Serres and at the foot of the mountains that form the border with Bulgaria, is among the most important in terms of both biodiversity and productivity. More than three hundred bird species visit or make it their home, fifty of them threatened or endangered. It also gives life to dozens of types of fish, reptiles, amphibians and mammals, including wolves, otters and Greece's last herds of water buffalo. Everyone agrees on its environmental significance, but this does not rank equally high on their list of priorities. Fishermen resent the competition from cormorants and

(above) Greece's last water buffalos graze near marshes of serene beauty
(right) More than 300 bird species visit or live on the lake

pelicans, farmers in Greece and in Bulgaria irrigate their crops – thirsty corn and cotton particularly – with its waters, and a sewage treatment plant has yet to be built to protect the lake from pollution.

Kerkini is unusual among Greek inland waters in that it is both natural and man-made. Formed when the glaciers melted after the last Ice Age, it gradually contracted over the millennia so that by Alexander the Great's time, the area was mostly swamp with two small lakes. Size made no difference to the millions of migratory birds travelling from Africa to the Arctic Circle and back. Periodic flooding by the River Strymon flowing in from Bulgaria brought nutrients to the district, making the soil as fertile as the banks of the Nile, and hardy farmers ploughed and tilled, inured to the bites of the malaria-bearing mosquitos that also thrived in the marshes.

These age-old patterns remained unchanged until the 1920s when 85,000 refugees poured into the Serres region from Asia Minor. Many of them succumbed to malaria and the government called in an American company to "turn the Serres plain into tens of thousands of fertile fields." By 1932 John Monks-Ulen & Co, the firm responsible for the dam at Marathon, had drained the swamps and the smaller lake and built a dam, diverting the Strymon into what became Lake Kerkini. Although hundreds of trees were felled or died as a result of flooding, the expanded but relatively shallow lake continued to be a haven for wildlife, unlike the reservoirs created in formerly dry valleys.

Fifty years later, the Strymon had dumped so much silt into the lake that the authorities raised the dam, trapping a good deal more water. In the process, they destroyed more trees and reed beds, turned more marshland into pastures, and eliminated the sandbars and mudflats where many birds nested. But again Kerkini differs from the norm because its water level fluctuates dramatically with every season. Between late May, when it's at its highest, and October, it shrinks by at least a third.

This is when the birds are happiest, poking in the mud for delicacies, lazing on sandbars.

Whole flooded villages stand exposed and tree roots attempt to dry out. Patches of lake turn flamingo pink, as those ungainly birds take over from the cormorants. In spring, though, those black divers easily outnumber all the other birds put together. And as our *plava* floats near the partially submerged willows where they roost, I'm reminded of a Naples slum, so crowded and noisy is this neighbourhood. Ebony-cloaked figures bristle from every branch, most of which support sprawling, twiggy nests. Raucous cries and clapping of wings pierce the still air, while white egrets and ibises jostle for position, feathers dangling like drying laundry.

We're being given a lake tour by Captain Yannis from Ecoperiigitis, a hotel/eco-tourism centre in Kerkini village, where virtually every telephone pole is crowned with a stork's nest. Since 1996, its founders, two other Yannis, Reklas and Avramidis, have been advocates for a logical water policy that will safeguard the lake's natural resources and keep farmers content, too. Yet they all say, as if with one voice, "Studies exist, programmes exist, but somehow the money gets stuck somewhere else." At the Kerkini Wetlands Information Centre, near the village church, Christos Kalaitzis also expressed his concern. The exhibition he presides over tells the story of the lake with beautiful photographs and diagrams, accompanied by texts in

Greek and impeccable English prepared by the ministry for the environment. "Where are the funds for flood control pumps? The lake will eventually die unless the water level can be moderated to keep the different habitats alive."

After the boat ride, and armed with a map of the area from the Information Centre, we took a slow drive around the lake, sometimes on the asphalt road, sometimes on the dirt track on top of the levee. While the villages ringing it are undistinguished, having been re-built after the devastating Bulgarian occupation and the Civil War, their gardens would do any English rose lover proud. And the countryside's lush fields emblazoned with orange poppies, stands of tall poplars and clusters of blue, indigo and vermilion wildflowers are almost as beguiling as the lake. We somehow missed Kerkini's most famous attraction – the largest expanse of water lilies in Europe – though locals said that even that has dwindled from 400 to 100 *stremmata* (40,000 to 10,000 sq. m) in recent years.

Back at the hotel, the sound of drums wafted in and out of our siesta. The Anastenarides or Fire Walkers were beginning the rituals leading up to their famous dance on hot coals on the night of May 21. Refugees from northeastern Thrace brought the custom to Macedonia when that region was awarded to Bulgaria after the Second Balkan War in 1914. But here in Kerkini,

one of the five or six places where they settled, the members of the sect also include Pontians, Vlachs, Sarakatsans and even Turkish speakers.

The official story of how this very Eastern-sounding practice started is that around 1250 the church of St. Constantine caught fire in the Thracian village of Kosti. Some villagers heard the icons groaning and rushed into the burning church to save them. They emerged unscathed, and ever since their descendants have com-memorated the event, some dancing with the icons, on the Saint's day and again two days lat-er on May 23. As they dance on the coals, stamping out all glowing embers, they also groan (*anastenazo*) in imitation of the suffering icons, which may be how their name originated. But the groans are those of rapture and not of pain. Not one of the initiates ever shows the slightest signs of scorching or even blackened feet, and no experts have been able to explain the phenomenon satisfactorily. Moreover, de-spite the ostensible devotion to the saints de-picted, the Orthodox Church condemns the practice, which appears to owe more to Dionysos than to Christianity.

Having heard about these legendary rites for years, I was thrilled at the prospect of seeing them up close. Their meeting place or *konaki* was next door to our hotel, so I spent the evening of the 20th in this plain, modern building,

An entire village – now submerged – was built on the banks of Lake Kerkini
for Theo Angelopoulos's film *The weeping meadow*, set in the 1920s

peering at the icons, which did not seem unduly old or valuable, and studying the people crowded into it. Six were musicians – two drummers, four lyra players – who kept up a steady, insistent beat and tune that never varied the two days I heard it. After a long prelude, an older woman uttered a cry and danced onto the rug, starting the ceremony. The dance too was simple, a few steps leaning to the right, then the left,

hands shaken in the same direction. Every now and then someone would kiss the two older icons and dance with them. The dancers, of both sexes, ranged from their twenties to venerably elderly. Some shuffled along prosaically; others threw themselves into the rhythm. In all, there were perhaps two dozen of them, but at least twice that number squeezed in to watch and the small room steamed up like a sauna.

The next morning the company set off from the *konaki*, pace still set by the musicians, to fetch a lamb to be sacrificed. When they returned, with two bleating creatures garlanded with flowers and ribbons, I confess I did not stay to watch.

We instead took ourselves up to the Bulgarian border, where I had a long soak in the Angistrou spa, reputed to have the best waters in Greece. Naturally hot springs pour into the squat Byzantine/Ottoman hammam, which has recently become incongruously attached to a modern, not quite finished hotel. Too hot to be truly enjoyable, it must have had a rather different allure in the days when the Turkish governor used to bathe there with his harem. A more spectacular Byzantine bathroom, with mosaic tiles and a high egg-shaped dome, exists at Sidirokastro, which is even closer to Kerkini.

Near the border, there are two other unexpected sights: the humongous Procom shopping mall, reportedly owned by telecom magnate Kokkalis, where you can buy everything from DVD recorders to the latest fashions by Kenzo, Lacoste, Nike… you name it; and the Rupel tunnel. Although open to the public only on weekends, the tunnel is actually 6,000 metres of underground city, built by General Metaxas in the late 1930s to defend Greece from Bulgarian invasion. Part of the so-called Metaxas Line, it was far more successful than the Maginot Line. The Germans failed to capture it in days of fighting, and after the fall of Thessaloniki in April 1941 made further resistance useless, they allowed its soldiers to withdraw with their weapons as a sign of their respect.

By evening in Kerkini, the drums were pounding again. But so were Zeus's thunderbolts. Stygian clouds were piling up to the west. Lightning streaked and blazed across them. Nevertheless, the Anastenarides piled up their logs, lit their fire and danced on, inside, waiting for the coals to form. Crowds gathered outside the *konaki*, more and more people pushed into the packed room. The tension was unbearable. The thunder got closer, the drums beat louder. Would they make it or had their fire dance turned into a rain dance? The rain god won. Half an hour before the coals were ready, they were deluged, drenched, drowned by a furious storm. The dancers filed out anyway, made a perfunctory circle where the fire had been, and returned, sodden and disappointed. Eventually the music stopped, platters of bread and lamb were passed, and we outsiders drifted away.

But don't wait until May to visit Kerkini. This paradise needs support from tourists. Let's show the authorities the lake is much more than a reservoir. ○

How to get there

Kerkini is 80 km from Thessaloniki, 35 km from Serres, and about 40 minutes' drive from the Bulgarian border post at Promachonas. We approached it via Polykastro, two-thirds of the way up the road to Evzoni and Skopje, where we turned eastward, passing Doirani, Kastanousa and Poroia before we finally spotted the right turn for Kerkini village. The trip from Athens took about seven hours, allowing for short stops.

Where to stay

Ecoperiigitis (Eco-tourist or traveller) in Kerkini and 1 km from the lake is both a hotel and an activity-information centre. Along with newly renovated, quiet rooms, a flower-filled garden and home cooking, its staff of experienced guides conduct boat, canoe, bicycle and jeep tours and can take you horseback riding, hiking and mountain climbing. A double room with breakfast costs about 65 euros per night (23270 51450).

Where to eat

Ecoperiigitis has an outdoor oven from which fresh bread emerges every day and where water buffalo, pork shanks (*kotsi*), roast pork and chicken are cooked in the *gastra* (a sealed pot) very slowly until the meat is meltingly succulent. The mountain village of Ano Poroia has tavernas in the plane-tree woods above it that must be beautifully cool in summer, and *To Gefyri* in Sidirokastro offers the usual grilled meats and appetisers in a pleasant setting next to a wooded riverbank. Some lakeside tavernas specialise in carp and catfish from Kerkini.

Unexpected delights in Drama

Nothing prepared me for Drama. I'd never read about it, never talked to anyone who'd been there. For all I knew it was just another provincial town, drab and uninspiring but an adequate place to break the drive back from Thrace to Thessaloniki. And a base from which to visit some of Greece's most illustrious vineyards.

As you enter town from the east, the streets are broad, and so are the sidewalks, a rarity in Greece. Several parks separate its low blocks of flats and sedate public buildings. To my surprise, these were dotted with gleaming marble sculptures, all modern, the work of

Nowadays the god of wine is again being worshipped in the Drama region, though bacchantes have yet to dance through its vine-covered hills pursued by satyrs.

Agia Varvara,
between the woods
and the water

artists from around the world who participate in Drama's Sculpture Month, hosted every May.

Our hotel bordered on a large park, with more sculptures, swathes of green and plenty of trees. We walked through it as night was falling, heading for Agia Varvara, where we'd heard there were some tavernas. With no signs to point the way, we had to ask directions three or four times, and invariably our interlocutors were cheery and helpful, whether they were older people or teenaged boys. In every case, they actually took the time to be more than polite. Is this normal or am I just a jaded Athenian?

Essentially a water park, Agia Varvara is a jewel any city would be proud of

Agia Varvara itself would be a jewel in any city. Surrounded by interesting old buildings – brick tobacco warehouses, early 20th century mansions with turrets, "Macedonian" houses with wooden balconies, a watermill turned into a restaurant, an art gallery – it is essentially a water park. Springs from Mt. Falakro to the north bubble up in this part of town, creating ponds, streams and islands connected by a labyrinthine network of paths. Trees of all kinds arched over them and over the water, some even grazing the rippled surface. Eventually our path brought us to the tavernas, lined up along a mini-canal. We could have been in Bruges were it not for the bouzouki jingling discreetly from one of them.

The springs and rivers in this corner of Macedonia attracted hunter-gatherers as early as 50,000 BC and gave Drama its name, which is a contraction of Ydrama, from Ydor (think "hydro"). More permanent residents arrived in the 6th millennium BC, settling at Arkadiko and Sitagri southwest of town. They left an exceptional wealth of artifacts and though cases of primitive stone tools, arrowheads and clumsy pottery usually leave me rather underwhelmed, the Archaeological Museum of Drama has displayed them so imaginatively and informatively that I could barely tear myself away. Maps, diagrams and texts in perfect English bring even the lowly hatchet head to life, while one room is a superb recreation of a Neolithic house with a hearth so cosy you could curl up in front of it.

The rest of the museum charts the city's history through equally attractive displays. There are hoards of Macedonian coins minted by Philip II, Roman statues and gravestones, a few early Christian and Byzantine reliefs and ceramics, and a splendid 19th century wooden ceiling with mythological motifs on an indigo background, which was lifted from a prosperous tobacco merchant's house. Opened in 2001, the Drama museum is easily one of the best small museums in Greece.

Many of the exhibits from the Classical and Hellenistic eras have to do with Dionysos, because Mt. Pangaion had an important sanctuary to the god that was one of the earliest in Greece. His followers were so exuberant that the area came to be known as *Idonida Yis* or Land of the Hedonists.

Nowadays the god of wine is again being worshipped in the Drama region, though bacchantes have yet to dance through its vine-covered hills pursued by satyrs. You would think that the area would be too cold for grapes. After all in Kato Nevrokopi just north of here the mercury often drops to record-breaking lows. But the district around Adriani, Agora and Mikro Hori to the east of Drama has a climate all its own, its gentle slopes protected from harsh winds, excessive humidity and sudden shifts in temperature. Nevertheless, although vines flourished here in antiquity, it was not until the 1980s that adventurous entrepreneurs thought of planting new stock and entering the wine business. The trend was set by Kostas and Nikos Lazaridis, marble magnates who control 45 percent of the Greek market. Their wines began attracting attention in the early 90s, and since the turn of the millennium another six so-called boutique wineries have joined them. As Yiorgos Manolessakis, one of the newcomers, says, "There's a competitive spirit in Drama, but it's to see who can produce the best wine, not sell the most."

If I was not prepared for the city's charms, I was even less aware of the magnificence of its two principal wineries. Both Lazaridis estates are showplaces and eons removed from the foot-stamped, resin-flavoured tradition of Greek wine making. These are high-tech enterprises but no expense has been spared to camouflage the fact. And neither gentleman could be accused of seeking a low profile. Both have enormous yet stunning estate buildings of a similar post-modern classical grace accentuated by colours of pale peach with a grey or terra cotta trim. Each spills over the crest of a low hill surrounded by vines. Wrought-iron gates, decorative stonework, murals, statues and, of course, glistening marble floors further the impression that these are palaces dedicated to wine. Nikos Lazaridis has even dedicated 4,500 sq. m of his chateau to an art gallery of the original paintings used as his wine labels. Not to be outdone, Kostas Lazaridis has given local architect Yiannis Nanos (who designed the Drama Archaeological Museum) the task of painting every magnum with a different motif, thus making them all works of art. Definitely not to be tossed in the recycling bin even when empty.

With so much emphasis on appearances, one might be tempted to suspect inferior wine, but nothing could be farther from the truth. As Chariton Maronikolakis, public relations manager

God's servant

at Domaine Constantin Lazaridi, guided us round the winery, he detailed the steps in the quest for quality. "You could say that conditions here are a bit too favourable, so we actually have to pare down our yield. This means that before the grapes are ripe, we have what we call the 'prasinos trygos' or green harvest and throw away 45 percent of what's on the vine. We aim at 700 kilos per *stremma* (1,000 sq. m) for our premium Cava Amethystos, 800 for red and about 900 kilos for white wine. All the grapes are picked by hand."

Drama lies shrouded in snow, a reminder that Mt Falakro, 45 km from the city, is Greece's northernmost ski resort

When you consider that this estate is the largest privately-owned active vineyard in this country, spreading over 2,000 *stremmata* (110 hectares), this seems like a Herculean undertaking. Annual production amounts to 1.2 million bottles divided among two lines, Chateau Julia and Amethystos, five types each, including the Cava and Fumé, using both French and Greek grape varieties.

Even more impressive was the news that California is Kostas Lazaridis' second biggest market. Half the production of Cava Amethys-tos goes straight to one of the foremost wine-growing areas in the world. They must be doing something right.

We padded through cellar after cellar, where thousands of oak barrels imported from France to the tune of $750 each lie undisturbed by any outside interference, unless it is their turn to be stirred, changed or emptied. But whether holding barrels or bottles, these cellars are elegant and decorated with paintings of mythical figures, as if the wines would benefit from their presence.

At the end of our tour came the ultimate treat – the chance to taste several of these elixirs. As I sipped, I wished I were holding an amethyst stone in my hands, since legend has it that the gem wards off inebriation (*a* is "not" in Greek, *methystos* is drunk), for the Merlot was smooth and seductive and Amethystos white is one of my all-time favourites.

After stowing a few cases in the trunk of our car, we drove on to the estate of Nikos Lazaridis at Agora, five minutes away. While the output here is about half as much as at Kostas', the impression is only slightly less grand. On the other hand, the pursuit of excellence seems even more determined, as if the elder brother were saying, "Okay, you're bigger and flashier than I am, but my wines are going to be better."

As his oenologist, Bakis Tsalkos, says, "Our wines, red or white, are not for immediate consumption. In Greece, the classic and the timeless must prevail."

In fact, the classic approach is taken to such lengths that the relatively new vineyards in Mykonos "listen to classical music"! In a more scientific effort to ensure excellence Chateau Lazaridi also subscribes to a quality management system approved and inspected by Lloyds of London.

Again we tasted, again we were beguiled, especially by the Chateau Lazaridi line. The es-tate's most valued red, Magiko Vouno or Magic Mountain never touched our lips. Named after Mt. Pangaion, whose gold and silver made Macedonia so rich in antiquity, it is apparently in such demand that each vintage sells out within a few days of its appearance on the market.

We finished our tour of the Drama wineroad with a visit to the boutique winery of Yiorgos Manolessakis, also at Adriani. Although he has only been making wine since 1998, from vines planted nine years earlier, he already produces seven types, 70,000 bottles in all. Here the installations are no frills, more what we're used to, but the wines are good, and so we loaded more cases into the car, thinking ahead to winter nights suffused in a warm winey glow. Our only regret, we just didn't have the energy or the palate to track down and sample the wines of Drama's other up-and-coming vintners.

But we'll be back, and not just for the wineries. Perhaps in winter to visit the ski centre at Mt. Falakro, or in spring to trek in the Rhodopi mountains on the fringes of the Fraktou forest, the only virgin forest in Greece and one of the last in Europe. But then again why not return on May 21 to watch the Firewalkers (*Anastenari-des*) at Mavrolefki or on July 20 to attend the Sarakatsans' annual gathering at Elatia? Drama deserves much more than our whirlwind tour.

How to get there

The nearest airport is at Kavala (Chryssoupoli), just 36 km away, which is served by both Olympic and Aegean airlines. Or you could take the train from Athens or Thessaloniki to Drama (OSE, 210 5240601). But if you're going to buy wine, you'll need a car. The city is about 2 hours' drive from Thessaloniki.

Where to stay (area code 25210)

We stayed at the comfortable, newly renovated *Xenia* (33195) in the centre of town. Outside town and closer to the wineries at Adriani and Agora are two new hotels, the *Tasko* (24000) and the *Kouros* (25800).

Where to eat

Who could resist a meal in the Agia Varvara park, sitting at one of the tavernas alongside the springs, under the trees? *Nisaki* is the smartest, with potted plants and flowers, liveried waiters and white tablecloths. It has been in business since 1962. We chose the more modest *Petros*, opposite, where we dined on Drama's famous grilled *soutzoukakia* (sausage-shaped meatballs), Macedonian pickled cabbage salad and superb roasted aubergines, split and sprinkled with a little chopped feta, garlic and finely chopped parsley. It was here that we first sampled Manolessakis' delicious *Yennima Psychis* red wine.

The Wineries

All the wineries are open during the week for tours and tasting. On weekends and holidays, one must call to make an appointment.

Domaine Constantin Lazaridi, *Adriani*, open 10 am-2 pm Mondays-Fridays (82231).

Nico Lazaridi, *Agora*, open 8 am-4 pm Mondays-Fridays (82049).

Yiorgos Manolessakis, *Adriani* (82010).

Wine Art Estate, *Mikrohori* (83626).

Others to look for: *Ktima Biblia Hora* at Kokkinohori, *Ktima tou Akropotamou* at Platanotopo, and *Pavlidis* in the Industrial Zone.

Kavala and Thasos:
lost jewels

In residence from 1391 to 1912, the Turks gave Kavala the name that has stuck, along with its most interesting building, the Imaret. The word means "poor house" in Arabic and, ironically, this has been the city's finest monument since Mehmet Ali donated it in 1817.

Kavala should be one of the most beautiful cities in Greece. Macedonia's second largest, it has all the right ingredients: a crenellated castle where an acropolis once stood, a natural harbour set in front of a steep hill like the orchestra below an ancient amphitheatre, some stunning architecture. If only its city fathers had obeyed that ancient maxim – μηδέν άγαν – nothing in excess. If only they had restrained the building of apartment blocks so that each row could have a view and some breathing space.

But history isn't written with ifs so one has to look hard to find beauty in Kavala amongst the thicket of "polykats" and incessant traffic. That said, its jewels shine even brighter for being unexpected.

One landmark needs no searching. You can't miss the aqueduct. Three tiers, 60 elegant arches, it winds through the city like a primeval snake. Suleiman the Magnificent had it constructed to take water up to the citadel, perched on the vertical promontory above the east side of the harbour. This was where Kavala

The Imaret is a marvel of Islamic architecture,
swirls and curls instead of Western right angles

began as Neapolis, a colony of Thasos and later the port of Philippi. For millennia its citizens clustered under the fort, within walls that surrounded the foot of the hill, no matter who ruled them. But nothing remains of Neapolis or of Byzantine Christoupolis, except in the (very good) archaeological museum. The flavour of the old city is Ottoman.

In residence from 1391 to 1912, the Turks gave it the name that has stuck, along with its most interesting building, the Imaret. The word means "poor house" in Arabic and, ironically, this has been Kavala's finest monument since Mehmet Ali donated it in 1817. Mehmet Ali's story illustrates the extraordinary possibilities for upward mobility in Ottoman society. Kavala's most celebrated citizen started life as the son of an Albanian farmer. He joined the Sultan's army and eventually wound up as Pasha of Egypt, where he founded the royal dynasty that ended with Nasser's revolution in the 1950s. One fine day he returned to his birthplace with his pockets full of gold and a proposal. "I want to help you," he told the people, "and I can offer you either a wonderful new port or a poorhouse with a soup kitchen."

His audience of suspicious fishermen rejected any change to their habitual waters and so Mehmet Ali had the Imaret constructed near the entrance to the old town. The result was a marvel of Islamic architecture, curves and swirls instead of our Western right angles and straight lines. Inside its walls he ordered courtyards, pools and gardens, a mosque and a library, barrel-vaulted arcades and rows of tin-roofed bubble domes interspersed with a forest of slender apricot-coloured chimneys. Although it also acted as a theological seminary, it came to be called "Tembel Haneh" – the lazy man's home – as it provided (in the words of the *Blue Guide*) "free pilaf and exemption from military service".

After the liberation of northern Greece from the Turks, the Imaret stopped functioning as such. A decade later it was housing refugees from Asia Minor but ultimately disrepair followed disuse. Old postcards show its walls as grey and dingy, its domes tufted with weeds. Guidebooks continued to extol its design even though only the exterior could be admired. Moreover, very little could be done to remedy the situation because, curiously, it is still owned by the Egyptian government.

One woman with a vision changed all that. For seven years Anna Tzouma-Missirian, a dynamic native of Kavala, negotiated with Cairo until she eventually persuaded the authorities to give her a 99-year lease and permission to convert the Imaret into a hotel. Twenty-two months later, it opened, and as I walked through its deceptively simple doorway, I left Greece behind.

In restoring the Imaret, Anna has spared no expense and every detail, down to the roses floating in a marble bowl, has received loving, tasteful attention. She imported antique lamps, bronzes and paintings from Egypt and Constantinople, her mother and a team of deft-fingered Kavalan women sewed the bed-linen and curtains for every room, pansies on the breakfast table match the pansies on the china, strawberries grown in the courtyard find their way to your room at night: all that is missing is Scheherazade to weave her stories or, if you're of the opposite sex, a harem full of houris.

Once ensconced in such sensual perfection, there seemed very little incentive to explore the rest of Kavala, but Vassiliki Karalioliou, one of the hotel's managers, herself from Thessaloniki, spurred me on with her descriptions of what lay behind the waterfront.

After the Sultan decreed in 1864 that Kavala could expand outside the Byzantine walls, its population began to multiply, from under 3,000 to about 50,000 with the influx of refugees in the 1920s. This sudden growth coincided with European addiction to the filthy weed. With its harbour so close to the plantations, Kavala became the tobacco capital of the Balkans. European and Greek companies opened processing plants, trading offices and warehouses. They lavished money on neoclassical facades painted in bright colours, Ottoman ornaments, Hanseatic roofs and even a down-sized version of an Hungarian castle with turrets and gothic arches.

Coming across these fanciful creations in the midst of the urban blahs is its own reward. The castle, white and charmingly absurd, houses the Town Hall; others have been revived as cultural centres or social clubs, while some are simply languishing, awaiting a new role. Echoes of what Kavala once looked like, it's a pity more of them were not salvaged.

Nevertheless, there are signs that Kavala is recovering from the post-war slump that decimated the city. As smokers switched to Virginia tobacco, the city's jobless had emigrated en masse. But now pedestrianised streets hum with shoppers, no café has an empty table, children roar around green parks and adventure playgrounds, high-school classes collect litter, and restoration works are about to start on the castle. We boarded an improbable blue and yellow toy train that connects residents and sightseers with the upper town and the waterfront, free of charge. Everywhere we went people smiled, with that jovial ease that you find so often up north.

Thasos

For many tourists, the only reason to go to Kavala is to pick up the ferry to Thasos, Greece's emerald isle. That's what we'd done sometime in the late 70s. Over the years that trip blurred into a pastiche of lovely beaches rimmed with trees, a mountain village that sold honey, and a golden eagle that coasted below us as we gazed over a cliff. So when we drove off the ferry and turned right for Limenaria, half way round the island, we didn't recognise much.

Before long, we realised that Thasos has changed. It is still green, despite a series of forest fires; its shores are still scalloped with chalk-white beaches, shaded by pines and fringed with irresistibly blue water. But what God hath wrought, humans are frantically trying to undo. Behind each pretty beach or little port stand untidy rows of garish buildings: pseudo-Bavarian chalets, rose-bonbon "villitsas", plasticised eateries… At Limenaria, the second largest village on Thasos, four and five-storey apartment buildings dwarf the few nicely restored neo-classical houses.

Disappointed, we turned inland to Theologos, billed as a traditional hamlet. Here venerable stone-roofed cottages are rapidly shedding their slate shingles for red tiles. "The government gave permission about seven years ago," said Anna Christidi, whose own new stone cottages above Limenaria look gracefully weathered. "Since then, people have been replacing their old roofs even when they don't leak, because tiles are 'modern'."

Nevertheless, Theologos' churches have been spared, their domes swivelling to a point like dunces' caps, the Local Products shopowners cheerfully open wine bottles and honey jars to let you sample, while the smartest café automatically serves mountain tea instead of Lipton's.

The next day we toured the rest of the island, looking for places we remembered. The beach at Limenaria should have made an imprint: three massive brick chimneys left over from smelting zinc and cadmium ore rise to the right of it; the Palataki, a similarly grand, late 19th-century building that held the mining company offices, straddles the hill between beach and port. Strange how the artefacts of early industry seem so romantic when abandoned.

Midway round this circular island, the scenery becomes more rugged, wilder. Viewpoint kiosks tempt drivers to stop and admire a monastery clinging to a cliffside or an enticing cove with no perceptible access. And finally we spied the place where we'd seen the eagle, barely altered.

Alyki, where you can swim in an ancient marble quarry

My favourite spot along this coast is Alyki. It's a strip of land between two bays. One side faces a wooded promontory and supports a couple of tavernas on a stony beach; the other contains the modest ruins of an Archaic sanctuary and some flattened basilicas. The real prize, however, demands a walk through the woods to the tip of the headland, where an ancient marble quarry lies partly submerged. Wind and waves have polished the stone into exotic, surreal sculptures above the neat rectangles carved just beneath the water's surface. A solitary column drum protrudes from amongst them.

Closer to town, we suddenly caught sight of the bare mountain peak, looming much higher than expected (1,204 m) for a smallish island. It seemed to invite climbers and I yearned for a jeep to take me closer.

Back where we began in Thasos town, also called Limenas (harbour), bits of Classical masonry and tumbled columns lie scattered unpredictably between modern buildings or under rampant roses. A stroll around the grassy Agora, where huge leafy trees eclipsed the marble; a climb up to the ancient theatre accompanied by thunder claps; a delicious dinner in a portside taverna while cataracts of rain tumbled around us – and I was ready to forgive Thasos for its architectural lapses.

Philippi and Amphipolis: an open and shut case

If you collect ancient sites, these are two outstanding reasons to visit the Kavala area. The Macedonian-Roman ruins of Philippi, closer and more famous, boast a grand theatre (which holds a summer festival), a dramatic basilica that towers over the agora, mosaics, baths and much, much more, together with whispers of St. Paul and the suicides of Brutus and Cassius, who lost the battle here for control of Rome to Octavian and Mark Antony.

But don't expect to visit the museum; it has been locked for the past ten years. Who can explain why? As an Englishwoman said as we puzzled over the jumbled stones with our *Blue Guides*, "I love the Greeks, bless their hearts. I bring groups here twice a year. But sometimes they're so frustrating. Some museums are always shut, others are Victorian, while a few are the best of their kind."

If I had known what I discovered later that day, I would have told her that the museum at Amphipolis, less than an hour away towards Thessaloniki, is among the best of its kind. It opened in the late 1990s with finds ranging from neolithic to Byzantine, but including gold wreaths and jewellery worthy of Vergina, delicate clay figurines, and the relief busts of a

In the steps of St. Paul at Phillipi

veiled woman, identified only as a "female divinity". Of extraordinary beauty and compassion, with downcast eyes, she looks like a forerunner of the Virgin Mary.

But when I asked about the site, Yorgos the ticket taker looked sorrowful and said, "It's locked… but I could take you round when the museum shuts."

Amphipolis covers a huge area. Without being especially noteworthy in history, it seems to have been particularly prosperous. Yorgos showed me a Hellenistic house with geometric

The old mining works at Limenaria

wall paintings, basilicas with mosaic floors portraying beasts, birds and sea creatures plus intricate kaleidoscopic patterns, ancient walls with special slits to control irrigation and, strangest of all, the wooden(!) pilings that supported a 5th century bridge.

Yorgos, who's just an employee, had the last word. "This country could live off its archaeological treasures if only it were better organised. What's the point of tourists coming to see them if they're always locked up?" ○

How to get there

Kavala shares an airport with Xanthi; it's located halfway between the two at Chryssoupoli, near the Nestos river delta and just a few kilometres north of Keramoti, where the ferry leaves for Thasos (45 minutes) at almost hourly intervals. Ferries leave less regularly from the port of Kavala, a longer trip. Kavala is also about a two-hour drive east of Thessaloniki.

Where to stay

Kavala boasts what must be the most original hotel in Greece. More than a hotel, the *Imaret*, which opened in 2004, is also a museum/monument of Islamic civilisation (2510 620151, e-mail: info@imaret.gr). Even if you have no intention of going there, take a virtual tour at www.imaret.gr just to see what a spectacular place this is. And when you're in the city, if your pocketbook won't allow an overnight, do stop by to have a drink or dinner.

In Thasos town, the *Philoxenia Inn* is quiet and set back from the waterfront. Its back rooms overlook roses and a lush vegetable garden. (25930 23331). At Limenaria, if you're in the mood for keeping house in pretty surroundings, the *Arsinoi* stone cottages (one and two rooms with kitchenette and terrace) on the hill above the beach on the western outskirts of the village could be pleasant (call Anna Christidi at 25930 52796).

Where to eat

Below the Imaret are several very reasonably priced fish tavernas. We chose the least noisy, very friendly *I Oraia Mytilini*. Future visitors may be able to eat at Mehmet Ali's house a few blocks from the Imaret. Anna Tzouma-Missirian also received permission to convert the old mansion with its garden into a restaurant. Situated next to Mehmet Ali's equestrian statue, it promises to be another landmark.

In Thasos, we ate well at *Palataki* in one of Limenaria's few neoclassical buildings and at *O Platanos* in the main town on the waterfront and next to the ancient agora. *Palataki* serves tender lamb raised by the family; the chef at *Platanos* makes a delicate stuffed squid. A local vineyard named *Yannakis* started bottling a very acceptable white wine in 2003. It is a great improvement on the Chateau Cardboard that has replaced the good old barrel wine of yore.

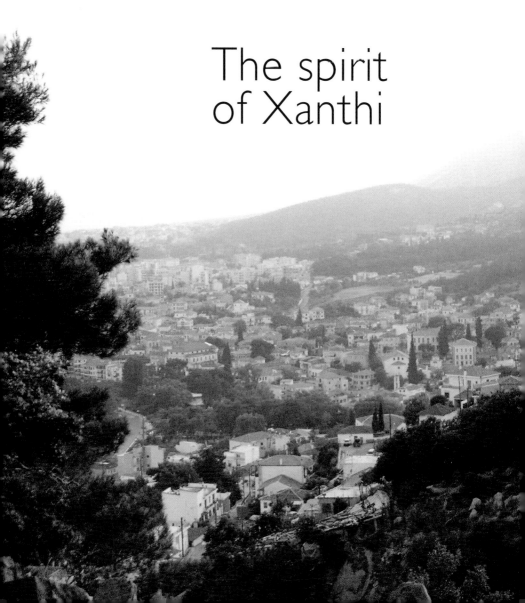

The spirit
of Xanthi

Under the Turks, Xanthi remained an inconsequential village until the late 19th century. Then a Franco-Ottoman company opened the Thessaloniki-Constantinople railroad. At last there was an efficient way to export the blonde Xanthi tobacco so popular in European salons and cafés.

Until I went to Xanthi in 1998, Thrace had been a long, narrow question mark on the map of Greece, teeming with Muslim minorities and tobacco growers. I knew it had produced Democritus and Manos Hadjidakis, but I'd heard no whisper of anything that could have prepared me for losing my heart.

It wasn't just that Xanthi's old district beguiled me with its prosperous pastel townhouses, cobbled lanes and total absence of commercialism. It wasn't the easy pace, fresh air and lush parks. It was not even the fact that traffic slowed down at zebra crossings, a double-scoop ice cream cone cost 250 drs. (70 lepta) and the grilled sardines were the best I'd ever eaten. I fell in love with Xanthi because it gave me hope. It's a corner of the Balkans where Greeks and Turks have not been ripped out of each others' lives by a population exchange or an artificial green line. On Friday I heard the muezzin call Pomaks* to worship in the mountain villages on the way to the Bulgarian border; on Sunday the priest's voice was twanging from the cathedral's loudspeaker. They did not sound very different.

At Xanthi's Saturday bazaar, which seemed bigger even than Heraklio's mile-long open-air market, Greek women in low-cut blouses and short skirts gossiped with Turkish women wearing dull grey overcoats and cotton head scarves.

They were both picking over tiny bright bikinis and sexy underwear. In the Pomak village of Myki, three glamourous divorcees had driven all the way from Katerini in southern Macedonia to consult its reputedly clairvoyant hodja about their future marital prospects. The little girls dancing in the café were as blond and blue-eyed as any Danes. Could they be descended from the Xanthians, the Thracian tribe that gave the district its name, which does indeed mean blond? In any case, a grizzled gentleman in a crocheted skullcap told me the Pomaks have been living in these hills for as long as anyone can remember, while Xanthi's population reflects fairly recent migrations.

Aegean Thrace has always been a passageway, a narrow strip of rich alluvial plain between the sea and the wild Rhodopi mountains, used by armies and merchants to get from the Bosphoros to the Thermaic Gulf even before there were towns like Byzantium/Constantinople and Thessaloniki. The whole area is littered with ruined fortresses and shrines from the prehistoric through the Ottoman era, not to mention abandoned World War II bunkers. Greeks from the shores of Asia Minor dispatched colonists there from about the 7th century BC, Samothrace ruled over parts of the coast in the days when its shrine of the Great Gods was one of the power centres of the

Mediterranean, Orpheus lost his Eurydice there and maenads drove men and women into drunken frenzies in what passed for the worship of Dionysos. Xerxes, Alexander, and a long line of Roman emperors marched soldiers east and west even before the construction of the Via Egnatia in the 2nd century BC. They were followed by Byzantine emperors, Slavic hordes, Orthodox monks, Jewish traders and Turks: generals, imams, bureaucrats and farmers with green thumbs. It cannot have been restful.

Xanthi did not have much to do with all this coming and going. Although Strabo mentions it in the 1st century BC, it was not heard of again until the 9th century when it had become important enough to have a bishop. By the 13th century, a Byzantine fortress dominated the hills above the Kosynthos river that flows beside what are now the northern outskirts of town. It was built to stave off Bulgar raids but failed to keep out the Ottomans. Under the Turks, Xanthi remained an inconsequential village until the late 19th century. Then a Franco-Ottoman company opened the Thessaloniki-Constantinople railroad. At last there was an efficient way to export the blonde Xanthi tobacco so popular in European salons and cafés. Newly rich merchants and plantation owners erected elegant, imposing houses, churches, schools, banks and warehouses. Some of these are in

Houses in the old district

and Greeks competed for the souls and property of the population. Slow rot had left the Ottoman Empire wobbling on very shaky foundations. Its end was in sight and nationalist emotions were seething in expectation of pouncing on the pieces. But four-and-a-half centuries of Turkish rule had left many Thracians sure of only one thing, their religion. Speaking Slavic did not necessarily mean you were Bulgarian; being Orthodox and worshipping in Greek described most of the Christian community. National consciousness had to be taught, and so began a fierce campaign to construct schools and dispatch dedicated teachers from Athens and Sofia. The highly politicised Archdiocese in the Greek capital and the Bulgarian Exarchate, which had become independent from the Patriarchate in Constantinople in 1870, sent agents to local parishes. As the struggle escalated, both sides were guilty of questionable ethics and unscrupulous violence. In 1912 Bulgaria, Greece, Montenegro and Serbia formed an alliance to throw off Turkish shackles. These unlikely bedfellows were successful and that is when Greece man-

stately neoclassical style, others bear the Macedonian trademark half-timbering and enclosed balconies propped up on wooden struts, the work of masterbuilders from villages near Kastoria. The Sultan fuelled the boom further by making Xanthi the district capital, and Austria-Hungary, Italy, France and Greece hurried to open consulates there.

Prosperity coincided with rising nationalism in the decaying Ottoman Empire as Bulgarians aged to win control of Thessaloniki – lining up troups at the edge of town just hours before the Bulgarians arrived. But the Bulgarians were not happy with the outcome. Ten days later they captured Xanthi and held on tight, with but two weeks respite in July 1913, until with the end of World War I, Allied and Greek troops finally freed the city in 1919.

Union with Greece in 1920 was followed by the incorporation of tens of thousands of new settlers from Asia Minor after the disastrous campaign to win back Byzantium. As one Xanthiot told us, "We are all refugees here." And in fact it's hard to locate someone whose ancestors were born in Xanthi, unless it's a Muslim. For in Thrace the population swap went in only one direction. While 390,000 Muslims were deported from the rest of Greece, those in Thrace were allowed to stay put in exchange for the continued presence in Constantinople of the considerable numbers of Greeks there as well as the Patriarchate. That clause of the Lausanne treaty was abrogated, violently, in 1955, but that is another story. In the meantime, demand for Xanthi tobacco plummeted, another war broke out resulting in another four years of brutal Bulgarian occupation, and Xanthi, together with the rest of Thrace, slid into a prolonged slump.

With the fall of the Dictatorship in 1974, its fortunes began to change. Thrace received its own university, with faculties in Xanthi, Komotini and Alexandroupoli; the 4th Army Corps was permanently based there; and money was poured into new factories to keep the population from seeking work in Germany and further afield. It was also designated as the new home for many Pontic Greeks from the former Soviet Union. Outside every major Thracian town we saw attractive workers' housing estates served by frequent free buses to the centre. "All they owe the Municipality is 10,000 drs. (30 euros) a month, and the apartment is theirs," our guide Vassilis Kapilidis told us, himself a typical inhabitant of Thrace with a mother from Crete and father from Ionia in Asia Minor.

Today Xanthi encapsulates all this history. But back in the old district, the keynote is youth. After classes and well into the night, students congregate on the "paralia". This word usually means beach or waterfront but in Xanthi it signifies the trendy music bars and garden cafés parallel to the Kosynthos river and opposite the Demokritos University campus and spacious Municipal park. One street nearby is the fastfood souk where souvlaki joints jostle with Goody's and Wendy's, but just around the corner a string of exceptional tavernas serves rich Anatolian concoctions like *yiaourtoglou*, flutes of fyllo wrapped around pastourma and cheese, smoked perch fillets and *tourlou riganato*. This

On the way up to Muslim Xanthi, the spirit of the East becomes more palpable

last is not the usual baked courgettes and potatoes but rather cubes of chicken and pork sautéed with tomato, mixed with a mound of fried potatoes and topped with a generous sprinkling of grated cheese melted quickly under the grill.

As you walk deeper into the Old Town, the spirit of the East becomes more palpable. Beyond the well-kept homes with painted façades, wrought-iron grillwork, and *sachnisia* – over-hanging enclosed balconies; beyond the 19th century square with its cathedral, school and ecclesiastical buildings, the streets paved with dark granite cobbles grow narrower and steeper, ascending into a district of small white-washed houses and modest apartment buildings. Here virtually every flat roof sports a satellite dish aimed eastwards, and two mosques with silver-tipped minarets are the most prominent landmarks. Small groceries stock packaged Turkish soups instead of Knorr and open jars of pungent paprika, crushed chili flakes and powdered cumin start you thinking about food again.

At the other end of town, barely 20 minutes south of the main square, are Xanthi's other architectural marvels – the tobacco warehouses. Grand three and four-storey stone buildings, each covering half a city block, stand abandoned and derelict for the most part. Windows shattered, doors sagging, they are still handsome examples of turn-of-the-century industrial design. A few are being restored, one already houses a senior citizens centre; they could be converted into splendid apartments. Beyond them soars the bright blue superstructure of the town's ultramodern new football field, and beyond it the sugar refinery, a 50s tobacco plant, and a host of other small industries that keep Xanthiots busy.

Given the region's turbulent history, there are plenty of reasons for resentment and distrust, but though one hears tales of unfair treatment by the Greeks and agents provocateurs sent by the Turks, these are generally speaking external factors representing politics not people. What the visitor sees in Xanthi today is different nationalities and religions eating at the same restaurants, working in the same offices and factories, shopping in the same markets; in other words, neighbours who have been getting along in the same territory for countless generations.

Back in 1998 I attended a workshop on this very theme. Members of the Re-evaluation Co-counselling Community of Athens spent the weekend with six Turkish women and four women from Xanthi. All our discussion was translated from Greek into English and Turkish and vice versa. Men and women, ranging in age from 21 to 60, from the US, Germany, Holland, the Czech Republic and Britain, as well as Greece and Turkey, we dedicated ourselves to breaking down the barriers that prevent people of any nationality, class or background from communicating, trusting and loving one another. Xanthi was the right place to start the rapprochement. The music playing in the streets could have been Turkish or Greek; the dance steps and movements were identical no matter who performed them; our meals which could have been cooked on either side of the Bosphoros were served by bilingual waiters. Where were the differences? What right have politicians to keep these people apart? On the last day when I saw every Turk at the workshop in the arms of a Greek, I knew they would find a way to get back together. ○

* For more about Pomaks, see the following chapter.

How to get there

Xanthi is served by the airport of Kavala at Chryssoupoli (32 km southwest of town). Both Aegean Airlines and Olympic offer daily flights from Athens. You could also take a long (12-hour) train ride, changing at Thessaloniki for the last 4½ hours, a bus or drive the whole 730 km as we did in the autumn of 2002. Xanthi has a few car rental agencies.

Where to stay (area code 25410)

We stayed at the quiet, clean and newly renovated *Orfeas* in the centre of town (20121). Other possibilities are the *Helena* overlooking the Kosynthos river beyond the park (63901) and the luxurious *Z Palace*, on the southern outskirts (64411-8).

Where to eat

A difficult decision because there are so many excellent restaurants and tavernas. We ate our most delicious meal at *To Ktima*, 4 km outside town on the road to Komotini, but were very happy with the Anatolian specialities at *Gonia* and *Fanarakia* on the pedestrian street in the vicinity of the National Bank building. *Kipos* in a garden near the river is a good choice in fine weather and locals recommended *Erodios* in an romantic wooden house in the old town. They also extolled the first two *bougatsa* parlours on Iroon Street near the main square, while the Oriental sweets and home-made ice cream at *Byzantinos Fournos* at the start of the old town linger in the memory. I should add that we never paid more than 20 euros for dinner or lunch for two and plenty of wine.

Exploring from Xanthi

From Thessaly to the northeast corner of Thrace, white fields stretch as far as the eye can see. They look as though a light snow has fallen, but the reality is more sinister: cotton is sucking this country dry.

A church in Rhodopi, practically hidden by autumn foliage

The office walls are a patchwork of photographs: people in sunny lifejackets paddling down the Nestos river in pink and yellow kayaks, trekkers wading through knee-high meadow grass and wildflowers, bikers peddling up mountain paths, water tumbling over a 35-metre precipice or slithering in an endless S through a green gorge. The desk is spread with albums showing more activities, more idyllic scenes and more happy nature lovers. But Antonis Dalakis, who runs Forest-land Adventure Holidays in Xanthi, looks out at the overcast October sky and says, "We can show you a lot of beautiful places but I don't advise kayaking in the Nestos right now. If it should rain, you wouldn't be very happy and there'd be no turning back."

We sigh and accept the next best offer, a train ride and a walk. Vasilis Kapilidis will be our guide, himself a native of Stavroupoli, a tidy traditional village about 25 km from Xanthi that is the region's ecotourism centre. The guidebook extols the train ride, so maybe it's a reasonable compromise.

The next day, Vasilis drives us to Toxotes, 10 minutes from the heart of Xanthi, where a sign proclaims the entrance to the "Aesthetic Forest of Nestos River Passage" and disappears inside the tiny, drowsy station there. He emerges with round-trip tickets for the hour-

Tunnelling alongside the Nestos Meanders

long journey to Stavroupoli and back. Cost 1 euro each. Eventually the dusty Alexandroupoli-Drama train pulls in, we clamber aboard and find window seats. Within minutes we're viewing the famous Nestos Narrows or Meanders, where for 20 km the river, which has its source in Bulgaria, snakes through lush low mountains and tufted grey cliffs. Bushy islands and bare sand spits, trees of all colours and stretches of browny-green water speed tantalisingly by us, chopped up by long seconds of utter blackness every time the train slips into a tunnel. In no time we've pulled into Stavroupoli and disembarked, only to find ourselves on the train heading back, glued to the window once more.

"Think of this short journey as an appetiser, a glimpse of what you might enjoy in fairer weather," says Vasilis, "I've taken 70-plus grandmothers and tots of 3 or 4 down the river. It's not dangerous at all."

Back at Toxotes, he drives us to the start of the path that parallels the river above the tracks and eventually winds up at Stavroupoli. Whether it is ancient as he says or merely old can be disputed, but it certainly has been carved out of the cliff and walking satisfies our craving to be active and closer to the sinuous river, though we still long to be paddling down it. Its banks are said to be home to 213 bird species and although we don't actually see anything but a few rock pigeons, we do hear some cackles, hoots and chirpings that betray their presence.

Some of these species are endangered, but so it seems is the river itself, despite its international importance as a bird sanctuary. Thanks to the construction of the Thisavros and Platanovrisi hydroelectric dams above Drama in Macedonia, water flow is erratic and its colder temperature has reduced the number of fish and birds in the Nestos. But the trouble starts even further north in Bulgaria, where large amounts of water are diverted for irrigation, and is compounded by additional intensive irrigation of thirsty crops on the plain between Chryssoupoli and Xanthi. In fact, wherever the ground is flat enough, from Thessaly to the northeast corner of Thrace, white fields stretch as far as the eye can see. They look as though a light snow has fallen, but the reality is more sinister: cotton is sucking this country dry and nobody seems to be able to do anything about it. Needing little care but consuming inordinate amounts of water, cotton is a favourite with farmers and a nightmare to environmentalists. Moreover, any attempt on the part of the government to change farming practices invariably meets with fierce opposition and tractor convoys blocking key roads.

On our third day, Vasilis takes us into the Rhodopi mountains, one of the least spoiled spots in Europe. At first we're driving through a rather unpromising mist but suddenly we rise above it, bursting into a sunlit day of piercingly blue sky, fir-tufted slopes, distant peaks floating above cloud banks and foliage so brilliant I'm reminded of Moses and the burning bush. This is the Haidou forest, home to brown bears, wild boar, deer, wolves, wildcats, none of which put in appearance, needless to say, but the beeches, willows and oaks put on a spectacle rivalling Leaf Week in New England. We pass immense woodpiles and small hamlets, Karyofyto — surrounded by walnut trees as its name implies — and Leivaditi, with about ten houses, a lodge and a taverna. Near here is the path to the famous waterfall, touted as the biggest in the Balkans. But we have to be content with glimpses of countless smaller roadside versions because we push on to the Dasiko Horio, a collection of new log cabins in a green clearing that look as though they've been airlifted from Yellowstone Park.

It would be a perfect place to get away from it all and walk to one's heart's content, especially as Vasilis says, "We want tourism with a conscience here, a few people who love nature, not caravans of picnickers leaving litter everywhere." There seems little danger of this occurring since the whole Stavroupoli district cannot sleep more than 100 people.

Besides extreme natural beauty the area has a few low key archaeological sites that lure visitors – a Macedonian tomb at Komnina, an ancient castle at Kalyva, the old stone bridge of Leonidas – but by far the most interesting cultural attraction of the Xanthi hinterland is the so-called Pomakohoria. These are the twelve villages due north of the city which are inhabited exclusively by a mysterious people called Pomaks.

These fair-haired, blue-eyed Muslims speak a dialect related to Bulgarian but which contains many ancient Greek words. Their history is so obscure that the three nations vying for their allegiance interpret it as it suits them. The Greeks believe that they are the remnants of an original Thracian tribe, the Agrianoi; the Turks contend that they are descendants of the Pechenegs, a pre-Ottoman Turkish tribe; while the Bulgarians swear they are Bulgars who were forcibly converted to Islam in the early years of the Ottoman empire. As for the Pomaks, they keep to themselves and if they know, they aren't telling. One thing is certain: they have been lumped together with the Turkish minority in Thrace for so long, that they feel more akin to their co-religionists than they do to Greeks. And, sadly, the Greek state has done little to win their sympathy. They do joke, however, that the women make wonderful wives, since they are hardworking and never grumble.

It is even difficult to discover how many Pomaks there are living in Thrace. The Helsinki Report on the Internet gives a figure of 30,000; Forestland's Antonis Dalakis, who teaches gym in a school in the border hamlet of Medousa, thinks there must be about 10,000 in Xanthi prefecture, 20,000 scattered between Evros and Komotini. There are other Pomak communities in eastern Thrace and in Bulgaria, but apparently they have little contact with one another. They also have no written language, and illiteracy rates are high, mainly because until a few years ago there were no textbooks teaching Greek or Turkish as a foreign language (Pomaks have had the choice of attending Greek schools since 1951). The men learn Greek in the army, but until recently the women in this very conservative society rarely progressed past fourth grade and had little contact with the outside world.

Part of the responsibility for this sorry state lies with a treaty designed to protect minorities.

After the exchange of populations between Greece and Turkey in the 1920s, the Treaty of Lausanne provided for equal rights and separate schools for Muslims, thus encouraging segregation. Junta decrees exacerbated the situation. Fearing possible allegiance to the Communist regime in Bulgaria, the colonels isolated the Pomaks within a military restricted zone. They required special passports to leave it and were forbidden to stray more than 30 km from their village. In addition, non-Pomaks had to have special permission to enter this zone, which was not officially abolished until 1995, while the travel restrictions still exist, on the books at least.

Marginalisation has taken its toll and Antonis talks passionately about other, ongoing abuses. "It's no wonder every house has a satellite dish pointing east," he exclaims. "They can watch Turkish TV for free. Whereas they pay for Greek TV – through the television tax included in all electricity bills – without being able to see it, because ET (the national television network) does not broadcast to the Pomak villages. The villagers of Myki raised money for their own antenna in 1999, and now watch Greek television, but the mayor of Ehinos is so alienated, he won't accept a drachma in aid for his constituents. To him, nothing's good unless it comes from Turkey." But television reception is a minor problem compared to the difficulties im-

A people with an obscure history,
Pomaks may be descended
from the original Thracian tribes

posed by the State in acquiring drivers' licences, owning property or government services.

The contrast between the Pomak villages and Stavroupoli could not be more pronounced. In Myki, Ehinos and Sminthi, the unpaved streets are muddy and rutted, many small apartment blocks are unplastered, while the only really cared-for building is the domeless mosque, usually painted an unexpected lime green or apricot. Plastic sheeting covers

Each village has its own distinctive dress

plaid aprons and headscarves. But they are shy and don't want to be photographed.

As we wander through Ehinos on our way to the mosque, I can hardly believe I'm still in Greece. While the signs above the small shops are in Greek, many of the graffiti are in Turkish. Bilingual election posters show candidates running on the Adelfiki Poreia/Kardeslik Hareketi ticket with names like Mehmet and Mustafa. Men with white felt skullcaps twirl worry beads outside a simple café, and a woman plucks my sleeve to show me her hand-beaded scarves for sale. For some strange reason the greengrocer has a large stock of pineapples and very little else.

Antonis says the Pomaks are not as poor as appearances might suggest and tells of an old man arriving at the bank after the new year with sackfuls of drachmas, some dating to before the War, to exchange for euros. Nevertheless the thought of these people without a history distresses me. If indeed they are descended from the original Thracians, they could be the group with the most legitimate right to existence in this land where practically no one can call himself a native.

But this is Thrace, beautiful and exotic, with a few issues that set it apart from the rest of this country, and which are both intriguing and troubling at the same time. ◎

many balconies and rooftops, turning these spaces into tobacco-drying sheds. Traditionally, the Pomaks are herdsmen or tobacco-growers, and every cultivable niche in the rocky landscape leading to these villages is planted with a type known as *basmas*, sought after by connoisseurs and four times the price of the ordinary leaf. Each village has its own distinctive dress, and the girls in Myki are the most fetching in their long black skirts and jackets, red and black

How to get there

Once in Xanthi, accessible by air from Alexandroupoli or Chryssoupoli/Kavala, you can put yourself in the hands of Riverland Adventure Holidays/Ecotourism (25410 64288, e-mail: info@riverland.gr; website: www.riverland.gr) or drive your own or a rented car. Riverland took over Forestland and merged with another agency in 2003. For real exploring a 4x4 would be ideal but most of the roads are asphalted.

Where to stay (area code 25420)

If you're taking day trips, Xanthi itself is the most logical base, but for a real retreat there are several options. In Komnina, the *Iniochos Xenonas* (22483) consists of self-contained bungalows sleeping four to six people with fireplace, fridge, TV and central heating. Also at Komnina, the *Nemesis* (21005) resembles a kitschy castle but it's as comfortable as a palace, again with a fireplace in every room. At Stavroupoli the *Xenios Zeus apartments* (22444) are possibility while the *Erymanthos Dasiko Horio* (21008) up in the mountains near the hamlet of Leivaditi. With two bedrooms each, kitchen, fridge, heating and fireplace, its cabins are apt to be fully booked on weekends. All these places are open year round.

Where to eat

Toxotes, at the entrance to the Nestos narrows, has what some people consider to be the best restaurant in the whole region. Called simply *Touristiko Katafygio Toxoton*, it looks unpromising but the food and service are wonderful. Our lunch came with an assortment of bruschetta spread with olive paste, red pepper paste and olive oil, which whetted our appetite for our grilled squid, grilled octopus tentacles and a sublime mixed salad, all presented with a quintessentially Anatolian sense of their aesthetic potential. There are tavernas at Komnina, Stavroupoli and Leivaditi, serving the usual mountain fare of grilled lamb chops and bean soup with better than average wine.

The coast of Thrace: from Abdera to Evros

Lake Vistonis is a bird
sanctuary and anything
manmade would take
second place to the
remarkable swirling
and plunging, preening
and flapping going on
just beyond the road.

After the heady mix of populations and
stunning landscapes in and around
Xanthi, the coast seems a bit of a let
down, at least to begin with. For one thing, it's
flat. And for another, it's empty. There's not a
soul to be seen in the streets of the small villages, no one working the cotton fields that end
in a white blur on the horizon. Even the flocks
of sheep are few and far between. Our first
stop is Avdira, ancient Abdera. This was the city
that gave birth to more than its share of famous
men: Democritus, the father of atomic theory;

The monasteries adrift in Lake Vistonis are more
photogenic from afar

Watch out for the pelicans sailing under this bridge

Protagoras, a leading Sophist; Anaxarchos, who taught Alexander the Great; Leukippos, another stellar philosopher. And yet, despite these brilliant sons, its reputation for dullness was legendary.

Moreover, Hippocrates railed against Abdera's unhealthy air, and as soon as we enter the unguarded gates to the overgrown ruins, we know exactly what he meant. Although we're well into autumn, the mosquitos are behaving as though it's a sultry summer evening and, to add insult to injury, it's only ten in the morning. Valiantly we march through the weeds in search of Roman baths, workshops and fortification walls but, frankly, the weeds are more interesting. This is a horta-picker's paradise and no doubt that is why there are signs warning against picking them. We have better luck on the acropolis opposite, where a Byzantine city called Polystylon sat atop the ancient foundations.

Here you can actually see the outline of a large basilica with an octagonal baptistery, a public bath complex and stout walls. But after a few more minutes of fighting off clouds of ravenous mosquitos, we retreat to the relative safety of the car, archaeological curiosity reduced to nil.

Only to be rekindled the moment we step inside the new museum at the village of Avdira, a few kilometres to the north. Within its walls, Abdera doesn't seem boring at all. Instead, the exhibits make the place come alive, which just goes to show what judicious juxtaposition and informative labelling can do. Divided into public life, private life and burial customs, the finds of Abdera depict a very human side of ancient civilisation. One display case devoted to beauty care, for example, contains not only all sorts of hairpins but also statuettes with different sophisticated hairstyles. Another contains tools: tiny spoons for measuring medicines, fishnet weights and hooks, knitting needles, tweezers… Even children get a case to themselves, filled with clay toys, dolls – including an amazing statuette of an African with monkey – counters for boardgames and little feeding jugs with spouts. There is also lots of stunning jewellery, some left as it was found in graves that have been reassembled.

The museum provides beautifully printed guides to its exhibits and to the site, in impeccable English, with aerial photos showing what we missed. As the Michelin people would say, "this is worth not just the trip but the detour," and it's free.

As we head east toward Alexandroupoli, it occurs to me that we are following Xerxes' path in reverse. The Thracian plain would certainly not have been empty then, in 480 BC. Herodotus says his troops amounted to 1,700,000 men, not counting camp followers. The *Blue Guide* revises this figure down to 200,000, but feeding this horde, no matter the size, would have devastated the countryside. There is a passage in Herodotus describing in detail what the army required, at the end of which an Abderan leader urges his people "to offer heartfelt thanks [to the gods]… because it was not Xerxes' habit to eat twice a day!" Ironically, many of the cities on the coast of Thrace were settled by refugees from Asia Minor fleeing Persian occupation.

By the time we get to Porto Lagos and lagoon-like Lake Vistonis we bivouac Xerxes and his soldiers to the back seat while we pay a visit to the two picturesque churches floating in mid-lake. They are connected by a wooden footbridge and, like many such photogenic settings, are best appreciated from a distance. (Corfu's Pontikonissi and Vlacherna Convent spring immediately to mind.)

But Lake Vistonis is a bird sanctuary and anything manmade would take second place to the remarkable swirling and plunging, preening and flapping going on just beyond the road. We pull over and creep through the marsh grass to a rickety weir where we can spy on what is quaintly signposted as the "herron collony". There are pelicans so large you think they are rowboats; white cranes stalking the mudbanks; terns, plovers, ducks and sandpipers in large numbers; herons, green and blue; and cormorants, looking like witches' capes spread over bare branches. It took us a while to figure out what they were; cormorants, unlike most water birds, need to dry their wings between dives.

One of Greece's most important wetlands, Vistonis is protected by the Ramsar Convention. After appealing for EU help in conserving the area, the Greek government then applied for and received EU structural funds to drain and reclaim 350 ha of land from the lake to expand cotton and tobacco plantations. Works were halted, thanks to efforts by World Wide Fund for Nature, the Greek Ornithological Society and the Royal Society for the Protection of Birds, but not before 10 million dollars of EU taxpayers' money had been spent. Where is the EU watchdog to make sure these kinds of appropriations do not occur?

Mesembria-Zone's intact storeroom

Back on the search for ancient cities, Maroneia presents a challenge. Even the *Blue Guide* admits "a full exploration of the remains requires time, determination and a knowledge of the literature." But there is a certain pleasure to be had in poking around unfamiliar spots, and I remind myself of a prize truffle hound each time we stumble onto a course of ancient or medieval masonry. Maroneia thrived from Homer's time to that of the Genoese, sur-

Though its identity is in dispute, the site is still delightful

rounded by 10.5 km of walls, sections of which can be glimpsed through thick olive groves. Discreet signs help, hinting at the existence of a mosaic floor, a theatre, a crumbling Byzantine fortress, shrines and a Roman arched gateway, all scattered higgledy-piggledy over a broad area. Tempting strands of golden beach nearby would be an additional reward in a warmer season.

Makri and Mesembria further east along the coast are similarly blessed, and the beautifully tended site of Mesembria needs no sleuthing skills. For archaeologists, however, this is a place with an identity problem. Most of them have come to think that it is, in fact, Zone, one of six colonies founded by Samothrace on the mainland. Herodotus called these cities "the walls of Samothrace", as they constituted a buffer to northern invaders. To the layman, however, the name doesn't make much difference, and what we like best about this site is its view and the wonderful spectacle of 129 perfectly preserved amphoras plunked upside down in an ancient storeroom.

After Mesembria/Zone, we join the much touted Egnatia highway to Alexandroupoli. So much has been written about this expensive new road that we are appalled to find long stretches with no median divider. Later, locals tell us that this will be remedied, but in the meantime its absence is inflating accident statistics.

Before we know it, we're driving through the broad streets of Alexandroupoli, the biggest town in this part of Thrace. It's pleasant as harbour towns are apt to be, but as a newsstand lady tells us, "There isn't anything old here. We did have one tall wooden building, the Pasaliki (Pasha's residence), but they demolished that too."

In any case, Alexandroupoli is a new city in this region of towns that date back to the 7th century BC but were abandoned even before the Ottoman conquest in 1453. It came into existence when the Orient Express tracks were laid in the 1880s, under the name Dedeagatch. This Turkish word means "Tree of the Holy Man" and has its origins in a colony of dervishes founded here in the 15th century. It did not become Greek until 1920, when it was first baptised Neapoli and then Alexandroupoli after a

Fishermen's huts blend into the Evros scenery

visit by King Alexander in June of that year. Its symbol, the lighthouse, was erected by the French while they were building the railway.

Otherwise, there is no reason to linger, and we do not even stay long enough to see what is reputed to be an excellent ecclesiastical museum. A night's sleep and we are off to explore the Evros delta, by far the most interesting area on this coast.

The colours of the marsh are almost as striking as the delta's birds

The Evros river forms the border between Turkey and Greece and the delta is within a military zone so permits are required and no one is allowed in unaccompanied. It is best to arrange your visit a day or two ahead through the Municipal Tourist Centre of Feres (25550 24310), and even then you may have to wait while they locate your boatman. It takes about one hour to drive from Feres to where the wooden boats are kept; the boat ride in the delta also lasts an hour and costs 53 euros.

At Evros, there are more ghostly echoes of Xerxes and his men. Although it is the longest river in the Balkans at 231 km, Herodotus claims the army drank it dry. If so, they were foreshadowing the modern Greek state, which drained a good portion of it in the 1950s and 60s for farmland, in the good old days when no one thought much about the environment and malaria was endemic. Even today the so-called flooded zone is dry in summer. As we drive along the arrow-straight causeway to the marshland, we see more cows than birds and even some wild, spotted pigs.

Another wetlands habitat protected by Ramsar, the Evros delta is one of the richest in Europe. Some 304 bird species have been sighted there, along with 46 types of fish, 7 amphibians, 21 snakes and 40 mammals, including jackals and wild boar. Like Vistonis, it is not without its problems, however. In this case, hunters are the worst offenders. It seems outrageous that they are allowed in this sanctuary and yet our boatman tells us that they slaughtered 2,500 ducks in the first two days after the season opened in September 2002. Not surprisingly, many other species flew off in panic. How does a heron or a flamingo know it's not the target?

The outcome is that we don't see those huge flocks promised in the brochures, which our boatman, Thanassis, says are so thick you can't see the water for the feathers. "Come back in April or May," he says. "There's sure to be lots of birds then."

Nevertheless, our ride in the delta is magical. There are enough birds – fish eagles, cormorants, cranes, herons – to keep us on the watch, and the colours in the mirror-like lagoon, the marsh grasses and even the scruffy fishing shacks lining the creeks keep me snapping the camera. As an extra bonus, driving back via a different route, we are able to creep up on more birds among the silvery puddles and cranberry-red grasses. Suddenly Thanassis says, "See that low hill? That's Doriskos. Where Xerxes reviewed his troops." According to Herodotus, who spends ten fascinating pages describing the various contingents and their armour, in addition to the soldiers there were also 80,000 horsemen, Arabians with camels, and 1,207 triremes. He singles out one admiral, Artemisia, a Greek woman from Halikarnassos, whose mother hailed from Crete. "None of Xerxes' allies gave him better advice than her."

With Xerxes and Herodotus for travelling companions, the coast of Thrace is anything but tedious. ○

How to get there

The easiest way to explore this part of Thrace is to fly from Athens to Alexandroupoli. Between Olympic and Aegean airlines there are at least three flights per day. Once there, you will have to rent a car since there are no bus routes to the ancient sites.

Where to stay

Improbable though it may seem, many of the resort hotels on the Thracian coast are open year round. Two of the nicest are at Maroneia. *Roxani Country House Hotel* (C class, 25330 41591) in pretty Maroneia village comes highly recommended for its setting, links with the Ecoexplorer adventure tourism office (25330 41550), organic produce shop and amenities The B class *King Maron*, on the sea, has a gym, sauna and hydromassage, among other offerings (25330 61346, 61348). We stayed in Alexandroupoli, where there are hotels for all wallets. The fanciest are the A class, 52-room *Astir* (25510 26448, 24571) and the B class, 102-room *Alexander Beach* (25510 39290), both at the western entrance to town. There are several more modest places nearer the centre, adequate for a night's stay, which is all you really need.

Where to eat

In Alexandroupoli, the *Mylos* fish taverna on the waterfront served us exquisitely cooked *tsipoures* (bream/porgies) caught with a speargun, tomato/rocket salad, and chilled Limnos wine and won our hearts with a platter of exotic sweets offered by Nikos, the owner. In winter, he moves to another address and adds spitted meats and Samothracian goat to the menu. Summer 25510 35519; winter 25510 84040.

For a lunch break between ancient sites, try the taverna above the tiny port of Makri. It has a view of Samothraki and several Turkish islands, and a menu listing dozens of seafood and local delicacies. At Agios Haralambos, near Maroneia, there are two promising fish tavernas next to an ancient jetty.

But when you stop for a coffee or beer at the Evros delta snackery where you'll get your boat, don't give in to your hunger pangs unless you're willing to pay Kolonaki prices for your sausage.

Dadia's vultures
and Soufli's silk

Dadia is often singled out as an environmental success story, or even "an inspirational example of ecoenlightenment". And yet it could so easily have been otherwise.

More predatory birds nest in the Dadia forest near the Turkish border than anywhere else in Europe. Of the continent's 38 species, twenty-one live there permanently; another ten are regular visitors. Yet this is not an area of inaccessible craggy peaks, as one might expect. Instead it is a patchwork of low, thickly forested mountains, open pasture, streams and exposed rock – in other words, something for everyone, mammals and reptiles as well as birds.

Dadia's most visible residents, however, are not handsome, charismatic eagles, hawks or buzzards. While you may spot one or two riding the thermals, the real star of this protected forest is the unglamourous carrion-eater, the vulture. Dadia is the only place in Europe where three of the four types of vulture breed, and the endangered Black Vulture population

has more than tripled, from 25 in 1979 to between 90 and 100 now.

Dadia is often singled out as an environmental success story, or even "an inspirational example of ecoenlightenment", according to journalist Mark Picard. And yet it could so easily have been otherwise.

Officially protected since 1980, the Dadia forest contains many of the ingredients for potential disaster. It is administered by not one but two ministries (development and agriculture), together with the WWF (World Wide Fund for Nature), the forestry department of Soufli and the local municipalities. Yet, the intragovernmental wrangles that are so often the source of mismanagement and ineptitude have somehow been avoided here. Funding has come from disparate sources as well, including the EU, MAVA Foundation for Nature Protection, Allianz group of insurance companies, and ELAIS SA, the people who bring us Minerva olive oil and Vitam. And instead of sabotaging efforts to protect the wildlife in this unique corner of Europe when they threatened their livelihood, the farmers and loggers of the district, and particularly their wives, are among the forest's staunchest supporters.

This did not happen overnight. The World Bank and Greek government were originally involved in a deal to clear the forest and plant it with fast-growing trees for timber. But in 1979 two studies sponsored by the WWF showed that Dadia was home to an unusually large number of birds, particularly predators, and also had the highest density of reptiles and amphibians in Europe. For once the animals triumphed. Development ground to a halt and the area was divided into two strictly protected zones separated by a buffer in which some grazing, logging and farming are permitted. But rather than abruptly imposing the rather drastic changes in land use, the authorities spent about ten years cajoling the people into acceptance.

Ultimately, it was the women who made the difference. As Georgia Valaoras, former WWF-Greece head, writes in a paper published online, "The importance of women in shaping local attitudes cannot be underestimated." As the Ecotourist Centre grew – from a vulture feeding platform to a hostel-restaurant-exhibition/information centre that attracts thousands of visitors every year – women seized the chance to change their lives. Even those with little education found jobs cleaning and cooking, while younger ones signed on as guides, lecturers and administrative or scientific staff. In 1994 the women formed a cooperative. Their menfolk were hostile at first, to the point of denying them a place to meet in the community. So they gathered on the steps of the church. Now 36 women run their own café-restaurant at Katratzides, a recreation area 9 km from Dadia village. And one in six adults works in ecotourist related activities. This is that rare rural outpost where young people have not had to leave to find jobs.

We saw them at work and at play the moment we arrived at the Ecotourist Centre on the edge of the forest one Saturday evening in October 2002. Despite the torrential rain, the café buzzed with young locals nursing frappés to a discreet beat, while women in their twenties handled all the comings and goings at the hostel and information room. They answered any questions not covered by the panels and brochures and gave visitors a slide show on Dadia programmes, to prepare us for the next day's excursion into the strictly protected zone.

Sunday dawned clear and sparkling, thoroughly washed by the deluge, and we caught the first minibus to the observation post to watch the vultures feed. You might think this is a bizarre way to spend a morning. You might also think it anti-ecological that humans have to provide scavengers with food, but there simply are not enough dead animals to go around any more. One programme recently approved by the EU will give WWF the funds to create ponds and clearings to promote the growth of the small mammals that raptors hunt as prey. For now, all the vets in the area cooperate with the Dadia staff, who collect cows, sheep, horses that have died of natural causes and take them (when no vultures are looking) to a remote plateau known as the feeding table about once a week. Our guide supplied binoculars and we took turns at the powerful mounted telescope.

Feeling like a voyeur, I watched some 40 Black Vultures and 19 smaller Griffon Vultures hopping about and jabbing at the carcasses. They are uniquely specialised: the Black Vultures, which have a wingspan of three metres and stand one metre high, tear the skin and attack the muscles; the Griffons, on the other hand, with their long necks are experts at getting at the softer tissues and viscera. Lammergeyers shatter the bones, Egyptian Vultures pick the meat off them; but neither species was dining that day. In fact, there is only one Lam-

mergeyer or Bearded Vulture at Dadia, and just another three in Greece, in Crete's Samaria Gorge. But the sight of a few cocky crows teasing and heckling the huge raptors sent any sad thoughts packing.

We watched the spectacle like Romans cheering on gladiators and then hiked back down to the Centre. Through pinewoods, over streams and skirting muddy patches, the trail was easy to follow and gave us a glimpse of more exotica, of the vegetal variety. Never have I seen such an ebullience of mushrooms. Red, white, brown, yellow, orange, pink, of all sizes – they were far more exciting than the one or two eagles silhouetted in the stratosphere above us.

Given more time, we would have spent at least another night at the comfortable Dadia hostel. Instead we drove through the semiprotected zone to Soufli, where much of Greece's silk comes from.

Soufli is dedicated to a phenomenon of a different sort: the silkworm. In its heyday a hundred years ago, the town's population was 12,000 people, double the present figure. It was known for its vines and its sturdy wooden carts, but whether permanently or part-time just about everyone was involved in the silk industry. Even the men helped raise the silkworms; processing the thread and weaving it were left to the women. In the 19th and early 20th centuries, Soufli was remarkably prosperous – a real success story – but union with Greece changed its fortunes. From being in the heart of Ottoman Europe, it became a border outpost, too far from Athens to matter much. And with the partition of Thrace in 1919, Soufli saw its most fertile mulberry plantations fall on the wrong side of the boundary line. The internal combustion engine made carts obsolete, phylloxera destroyed the vines and, after the Second World War, nylon and synthetics slashed demand for silk.

Today Soufli soldiers on in a time warp. Its shops seem to offer nothing but silk in all its guises; the chief souvenir is a set of worrybeads made of felt-like white cocoons; virtually all the women work in the local silk factories and they still raise silkworms in their homes. But many of the grand old brick and timber cocoon houses are derelict and a shop assistant told me she earned only 100,000 drs a month (294 euros). "I can't afford to leave home," she said, "and the young people move away. There aren't enough jobs to go around."

But nobody who loves fine silk should miss a visit to Soufli. The prices are reasonable, the workmanship unsurpassed, whether you're looking for a shirt or a bedspread. Although a few shops also double as museums, for real insight into how silk used to be made there is no substitute for the Soufli Silk Museum itself, unique in Greece. Occupying the splendid old Kourtidis mansion, the exhibition is divided into the history of silk from China on, the rearing of silkworms, processing silk from cleaning the cocoons to weaving, and the history of Soufli – most of it presented through photos captioned with fascinating facts. For example: One cocoon will produce up to 2.5 km of thread; it takes 1,000 kg of mulberry leaves to rear a box containing just 26 g of silkworm eggs over a period of forty days; and "one such box will produce 60-70 kg of raw cocoons, which in turn yields 20-30 kg of desiccated cocoons, eventually yielding 3-4 kg of silk yarn." When you consider that each thread is only 0.00005 m thick, surely Soufli produces enough silk to wrap the world many times over. The mind boggles.

Sunday lunch at Lagotrofeio taverna outside Soufli gave us a different perspective on life in this remote corner of Greece. Half the town seemed to be attending a baptism party. No one was wearing silk; none of the younger women were wearing skirts – stylish pantsuits and calf-length cardigans were the fashion; and not a single pickup was parked among the Audis, Mercedes, and Alfa Romeos. There's more to Soufli than meets the eye. I think there may be another success story in the making here. ⭘

How to get there

The Dadia-Lefkimmi-Soufli forest is about 70 km from Alexandroupoli, which is served by both Olympic and Aegean airlines. For exploring this part of Thrace, you really should have a car, and there are car hire agencies in the city.

Where to stay (area code 25540)

The *Dadia Ecotourist Centre* operates a simple but comfortable pension with 20 rooms (100 beds) on the outskirts of the park. At 39 euros for a double room per night, including breakfast at the snack bar, it's the best value in Thrace, and would be a fine base for visiting the Evros delta and Didymotei-cho, too. It's advisable to reserve in advance, especially on weekends (32263). In Soufli there are two options, the new *Municipal Hostel* (*Dimotikos Xenonas*) in an old cocoon house (22400) and the cosy little *Orfeas* with 20 rooms in the centre of town (22305).

Where to eat

You can get snacks, cold cuts and *saganaki* (melted cheese with ham and tomato) at the Dadia cafeteria, while the village of Dadia has a few tavernas serving the usual grilled meats and salads. Four kilometres east of Soufli (coming from Dadia) the *Lagotrofeio* taverna cum game farm serves hare and venison raised on or near the premises, cooked in *stifado* or red sauce (*kokkinisto*). Other meats are available, and *mezedes* include cheese fritters, wild greens with garlic sauce (*skordalia*), while the *moustalevria* (grape must pudding) offered on the house was the best we'd tasted in eons. We drank *Bellos*, a very decent Soufli wine, wherever we went.

Didymoteicho and Komotini

The woman in the Didymoteicho vegetable shop looked at me in disbelief. "You're from Athens! Nobody ever comes up here. They've forgotten us."

Wrongly. If this town were closer to Athens, it would be on every tourist's itinerary. People would flock to inspect its twin-walled castle, its mosques and churches; cars would sport I♡ Didymoteicho stickers; and its sausages would be featured on menus round the country. And no doubt it would have lost something in the transition from outpost to mainstream sight.

One reason for the town's appeal is that it was not always on the fringes of history. When

Ironmongers hammer hot metal, skull-capped tailors peer at their needlework in blackened workshops, confectioners dip threaded walnuts into thick syrup, while the aroma of freshly roasted chickpeas floats through the whole marketplace.

Didymoteicho's twin walls, strong in places, crumbling in others

the Roman emperor Trajan renamed the Greek city of Dyme after his wife, Plotina, it became a booming trading post between Trayanoupolis on the coast and Hadrianopolis (now Edirne) further north. A gold life-sized bust of Septimus Severus in the Komotini museum shows just how much wealth must have been floating around back then. Later, after Plotinoupolis was christened Dimotika, two Byzantine emperors were born here and another crowned himself (after Constantinople had fallen to the Franks); Frederick Barbarossa captured the city during the Third Crusade; and a curious inscription next to a crumbling dun-

Ruined hamman near the twin walls

geon below the fortress mentions that Charles XII of Sweden was imprisoned here by Sultan Ahmed III in 1713.

The town's most imposing religious building is Turkish, a grey-stone mosque 1,000 m square with a pyramidal roof – not a dome – started by Murad I and finished by his son Bayezit in 1402. One of Europe's largest, the mosque is locked now, despite Didymoteicho's consider-

able Muslim population. This is, of course, another source of interest. Thirty percent of its 8,500 townspeople are of Turkish origin; some villages have no Christians at all. The largest supermarket is Consum, not Sklavenitis.

"But pay no attention to what you read in the papers," another Greek shopowner told me. "There's no animosity between us here or across the border. I go to Turkey all the time."

The mosque dwarfs Didymoteicho's other buildings

There are also indications that people in authority are remembering Didymoteicho at least on occasion. The main shopping streets are newly cobbled, a smart café with plush couches instead of rush-bottomed chairs straddles the steps beside the mosque on the central square, and the famous walls are lit up at night. Symbols of military might – a tank, a fighter jet poised for take-off – strike an incongruous note at other squares, reminding friend and foe that this is a border town at the ready. And, like other Thracian cities, brand new model workers' housing units stand on the outskirts.

But Didymoteicho still lacks polish. Some will find this scruffiness genuine and exotic, others will complain that its monuments deserve better care. The weathered brick of a collapsed Ottoman *hammam* lurks behind a bakery near the square, begging for restoration. Another baths complex, in better condition, overlooks the Erythropotamo (Red River) on the south side of town. These used to be called the Baths of Love, for their air ducts are said to have rustled with the passionate whispers of young men and women lacking other means to communicate. The baths, mosque and Imaret or poor house went up outside the fortress, where the Christians lived.

The fortress or upper city, though neglected, is also romantic. Encircling a low hill, a blip on the flat plain stretching to the Evros river, the three-gated walls with their ten towers and bastions enclose two Byzantine churches, cisterns, storerooms and windmills, not to mention several rapier-like aerials. Cypresses and pines crowd the spaces where homes once stood, but even today some of the half-timbered houses inside are still occupied. Here and there the dual character of the walls – ancient and Byzantine – is strikingly obvious, but who knows precisely when Dimotika changed its name again, to Didymo (twin) Teicho (wall)?

No matter which part of town you're in, however, it is lively and the people are friendly; particularly the butchers, of which Didymoteicho has more than its share. This must be the sausage capital of Greece. On election weekend in October 2002, long links of pink, red and grey

wurst hung like grotesque beaded curtains in front of each shopwindow, blocking out the sunlight. Perhaps more were made than usual to cater for out-of-towners who'd returned to vote. A steady stream of customers from little old ladies to stalwart men beamed broad smiles as they grappled with packages of 5 kg and more to take back to Athens and Thessaloniki. A taste of home; what better souvenir?

Komotini

The drive from Didymoteicho to Komotini, Thrace's other town with a large percentage of Muslims, is one of the most stunning in Greece. Were it not for a smattering of cotton fields, its lower hills and trees could be in southwest England. Beyond Metaxades, a hamlet built of stone, the hills grow higher and cultivated plots give way to oak forests. For miles on end, we saw no sign of habitation; even cars were a rarity. More common, ominous signs warned against taking photographs, the only evidence that guard posts hidden behind the brilliant foliage were keeping close watch over the Bulgarian border in the haze to the north. We stopped to chat with a lone Muslim shepherd on a curve above an emerald valley, and eventually tobacco plants hinted that there were Pomaks in the area.

In the café/shop in Megalo Dereio, a Pomak

Komotini, two cities in one

village, a young Greek woman who'd come back from Drama to cast her vote made us a coffee, while two Muslim men told us in halting Greek that the reason why we hadn't noticed mosques in the countryside is that minarets require a costly building permit. Without spires to distinguish them, flat-roofed Thracian mosques blend into the background.

There's no mistaking the mosques in Komotini, however. This city of 40,000 people has sixteen of them, all open, with shapely domes and elegant, often silver-tipped minarets. It also has opulent neoclassical mansions with pastel facades, students attending the University of Thrace, remnants of Byzantine wall, a metalworkers souk, the largest open-air bazaar in Northern Greece, Macedonian-style buildings and a shanty town. Komotini – Koumoutzina to its Byzantine founders, Ghioulmoutzina to its Ottoman conquerors – is two cities in one, divided down the middle into Muslim and Christian, Turkish and Greek.

The largest bazaar in Greece

As provided by the Treaty of Lausanne which dictated the terms of the population exchange of the 1920s, the ethnic Turks have their own elementary schools and learn Greek as a foreign language. Many children drop out even before 6th grade, and the existence of only two Turkish-language high schools – one in Komotini, the other in Xanthi – has meant that few attend, and even fewer go on to university. The men perfect their Greek when they do their national service, without weapons training; the women often don't speak it at all.

Mustapha Mustapha, a pathologist and former MP, sends his daughter to university in Istanbul, as do many other Muslims with means. But he said that, though limited, the 1996 ruling that 0.5 percent of the student body at every Greek university must be Muslim has enhanced prospects for higher education. A soft-spoken, genial man, Mustapha received us in his office/laboratory in a dingy building up a narrow street in the Turkish quarter.

"No, I can't say I feel Greek," he told us, "but with the improvement in Greek-Turkish relations, there has been a real improvement as regards discrimination against us. The atmosphere has changed for the better."

As Foteini Tsibiridou, an anthropologist who was born in Komotini and teaches there today, explained, "We grew up playing together until we were about fifteen. Then we stopped because we knew we couldn't fall in love. Muslim-Orthodox marriages do happen, but the couple has to move away. Neither society would accept them here.

"Cyprus changed how children played," she went on, "but I have to tell you that as far as business is concerned, Greeks and Turks have always gotten along beautifully and true friendships develop between them."

This mix of cultures is Komotini's chief appeal to a visitor, all the more so because of its location in a flat, featureless plain. Modern shoebox apartments have replaced lots of traditional dwellings, making the Greek districts less colourful than they were ten years ago. The Folklore and History Museum in a restored three-storey house represents a very successful attempt to take us back a hundred years: to handcrafted wooden staircases, stained glass windows, elaborate embroideries and rustic farming equipment. The excellent Archaeological Museum took us much further back to prehistoric cave etchings and Greco-Roman masterpieces from Mesembria-Zone and Maroneia. But somehow we kept straying to the other side of that dividing line, Ermou Street, where the past is still present.

Though beautifully exhibited, we'd seen artifacts like those before. It was life we were after. And the Turkish district is teeming with it. Gone are shopwindows, goods displayed neatly behind glass. Here wares piled higgledy-piggledy, spilling into the streets or dangling from low ceilings, inviting rummaging. Ironmongers hammer hot metal, skull-capped tailors peer at their needlework in blackened workshops, confectioners dip threaded walnuts into thick syrup, while the aroma of freshly roasted chickpeas floats through the whole marketplace. Komotini is famous for these *stragalia*, a preferred movie snack before the days of popcorn and cheese-coated nachos. We bought sackfuls of thick sesame-coated *pastelli*, bite-sized *loukoumia* scented with rosewater, and one of those long walnut sausages, *soutzouk loukoum*.

Back on the Greek side of Ermou Street, I watched the flow of people. Men of both cultures crossed the unofficial border, women in headscarves rarely did. But a bevy of Muslim

Man-made and natural beauty west of Komotini

teenagers, wearing stretchpants and belly-revealing tops, sat down at one of the cafés hemming the massive main square, as brazen as any Greek girls. According to Foteini Tsibiridou, it's the dress code – the overcoat and covered head – that keeps Muslim women isolated and shy, at home and in their own neighbourhoods. With more children attending Greek public schools, this too is sure to change. But let's hope Komotini holds onto its other traditions for a while longer.

West of Komotini, on the road to Xanthi, the village of Iasmos in the Rhodopi foothills is half Christian, half Muslim. It has a Christian mayor, a Muslim deputy mayor. Near it a three-arched stone bridge of indeterminate age crosses a river rushing through dramatic scenery. Iasmos could be a symbol for the allure of Thrace: natural beauty, fascinating cultures, and the conviction that they don't have to clash. ◯

How to get there

The closest airport is Alexandroupoli, where you can hire a car. Didymoteicho is 94 km from this coastal town, Komotini 59 km. The drive between them can take a few hours or all day depending on your route and where you stop.

Where to stay

In Didymoteicho we stayed at the new *Hermes* hotel not far from the famous walls, on the road to Metaxades (25530 20250). In Komotini the *Astoria* (25310 35054), a red-trimmed neoclassical building on the main square, and the *Olympus* (25310 37690), a recently renovated hotel near it, are well placed for exploring the city on foot. Both are B class.

Where to eat

We had two of our finest meals of the Thracian trip in Didymoteicho and Komotini. *Klimataria* (on the main road just north of the Didymoteicho hospital and the Town Hall) had wonderful local specialities, such as *sarmadaki* (liver, rice, spring onions and mint wrapped in caul and tasting of Easter), pickled cabbage, five types of delicious sausage and *kavourmas* (pork roll tasting like the French *rillettes*). In Komotini *To Petrino aka Petrinos Toichos* had fish dishes worthy of one if not two Michelin stars. We feasted on tiny shrimp *saganaki* with a touch of feta and hot pepper and two splendid soles, one fried meunière, the other steamed with a delicate lemon and parsley sauce. The owner, a Muslim, said it was a secret recipe.

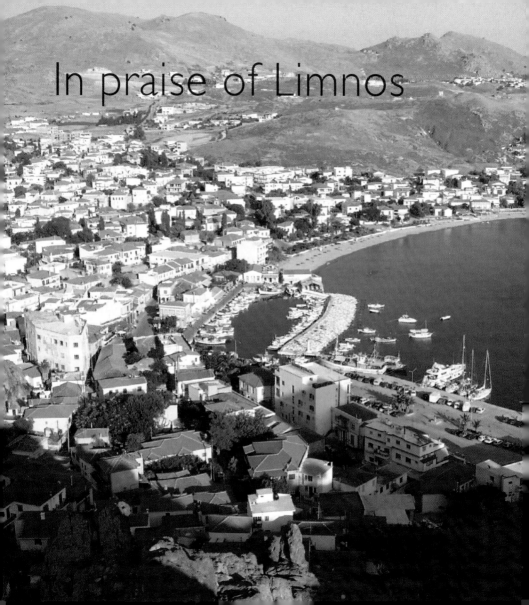

In praise of Limnos

Sixteen layers of habitation phases have been exposed here, going back to the fifth millennium BC.

Some places suffer from bad press. This can be a good thing. You set off with low-ered expectations and wind up being pleasantly surprised. So I wasn't at all deterred when a friend said, "Why on earth do you want to go to Limnos? It's boring, there's so little to do that after a day or two tourists hang around the airfield waiting for the F-16s to take off."

It's true that one reason why Limnos hasn't made a huge splash on the tourist market is the prejudice against its use as a major military base. Greece's eighth largest island, shaped like a lop-sided butterfly, lies near the entrance to the Dardanelles and as a result boasts nearly as many army camps as villages. But their camou-flaged huts are not obvious from the main roads and the soldiers circulate discreetly in

Myrina, the so-called "Turkish Beach", beyond the inner and outer ports civvies. In any case, I for one have never been put off by the presence of cute guys with crew-cuts.

Another prejudice against the island stems from the fact that it is agricultural. So, maybe it does look like the western edge of the Great Plains, with stubbled squares of wheat and barley carefully marked out on flat valleys that ease into hills as gentle as a camel's hump. Trees may be scarce, too, but considerable patches of intense green brighten up the landscape. And knowing that Limnos has been the breadbasket and wine barrel of the Aegean since the Bronze Age and probably earlier is reassuring in its continuity. Traditional livelihoods have gone the way of the dodo on so many other islands that tilled fields or active farms are almost curiosities these days.

Arriving bleary eyed at the ungodly hour of 6.30 am, we picked up a car at the airport with a warm welcome from Vassiliki of Petrides Tours and drove straight to Myrina, thinking only of going back to bed. The sight of the town sent sleep packing. Jagged black volcanic rocks tower over the white waterfront, the larger one looped with a castle. Begun by Byzantines in 1186 on top of foundations laid twenty-four centuries earlier, the gap-toothed crenellations on the meandering grey walls look absurdly like the starched trim on an irregular tablecloth. Ge-

noese, Venetians and, of course, Turks added to and subtracted from the design, while the fort gave a second name to Myrina.

When my husband first came here on October 10, 1944, he knew it as Kastro. The town was much smaller then, the port a fraction of the size it is now. And the war was drawing to a close. Still in his teens, he was part of the force sent to liberate Limnos from the Nazis. They'd exchanged their fleet tender for a large kaiki in Lesvos and sailed up without the protection of big guns, not expecting much opposition. The enemy had already been beaten and most of the Germans had fled the island.

They had not reckoned on being taken for the enemy themselves. As they tied up on the inner mole, now chockablock with fishing boats, scowling faces appeared from behind every window facing the pier. What was worse, every man was pointing a rifle right at the kaiki. "Communists," muttered H's commanding officer, "I'll go talk to them. Wait here."

Of course, they waited, frozen on deck with their own rifles aimed back at their countrymen. It must have taken a couple of hours for their officer to defuse the situation, but felt like the proverbial eternity. Who knows what was said, but after that rounding up the Germans was boy scout work.

Not a whisper of such grimness lurks in My-

As they tied up on the inner mole, now chockablock with fishing boats,
scowling faces appeared from behind every window

rina today. Taverna tables cover almost every inch of the inner port, set in front of low, blue-shuttered buildings. Tourists and locals throng the back streets, where fashions for matrons, sequined slippers, light fixtures, wine, cheese and sweet displays far outnumber souvenirs and beachwear. The architecture is a medley of picturesque Turkish with overhanging balconies on struts, elegant neoclassical, and unpretentiously ordinary. In short, it's that rarity – a thriv-

ing, unspoilt island town. I make a mental note to return to the food shops.

Restored by a catnap, we take the next step in retracing H's past and drive to Moudros. For such a huge, sheltered bay that is one of the best anchorages in the eastern Mediterranean, Moudros has remarkably little to say for itself. Cranes and egrets wade daintily in its marshes, the port boasts a brand new, empty marina and broad, empty piers, a garden café looks out to sea. Exploration round the back reveals a cluster of derelict stone buildings. H was billeted in one of them for two months while he and his mates looked after their captive Germans, who had erected them in the first place. Here he discovered a cache of food and managed to divert some of it to his parents in starving Athens. He was listening to the radio here when the Germans surrendered to the British on October 14.

Memories sneak back to him. But there are so many memories hovering unobtrusively round Moudros. Near the café a bust of Admiral Koundouriotis commemorates the end of the Ottoman occupation in 1913. A bronze plaque near the pier describes the events of just two years later, when the British used the bay to mount Churchill's catastrophic campaign against Gallipoli only 110 km away. A map shows the location of the eleven temporary hospitals set up to care for the wounded; two hundred ships had gathered here to launch the attack. Outside Moudros, sober stone gates frame the entrance to the East Mudros Cemetery where almost 900 Commonwealth soldiers lie buried under square slabs, some without a name. They are just a fraction of those who perished. Although Alan Moorhead wrote that "a day at Gallipoli was worth a lifetime in the Outback," thousands never got the chance

to be buried. The campaign, which settled nothing, cost the lives of 44,000 allied troops (including 8,000 French) and 86,000 Turks.

We pay our respects and head south to Poliochni, which puts things in perspective. Here, not far from the sea, low ochre stone walls demarcate paved streets, square houses and the advanced plumbing (a stone bathtub) of the first city on European soil. Higher walls enclose the public granary, an oval set of tiered benches shows where the town council met. Sixteen layers of habitation phases have been exposed here, going back to the fifth millennium BC. It was contemporary with Troy, but vanished in 2100 BC, destroyed by an earthquake, long before Agamemnon & Co set out for Helen.

But maybe this was where many of Limnos's myths are set. Could it be that Hephaistos had his forges here? He'd landed on the island when Hera, never one to spare the rod, tossed him out of Olympos for meddling during one of her legendary squabbles with papa Zeus. The name suggests it and the Limnians were among the earliest bronze workers.

Perhaps it was here that the Argonauts landed. They couldn't have arrived at a better moment. It seems that the women of Limnos had somehow angered Aphrodite who retaliated by imbuing them all with a most unladylike stench. This repulsed their men, who sailed off

The splendid Greco-Roman theatre at Hephaistia, unveiled in 2005, is a must

to Thrace to find more salubrious wives. When they returned, the scorned hellions murdered them all. Presumably Jason and his pals knew nothing of this and the stink had worn off. They were welcomed so enthusiastically that several forgot about the Golden Fleece and stayed on as husbands. Archaeologists call this the Thessaly Connection, mythical evidence of trading ties between prehistoric Iolkos (near today's Volos) and Limnos.

Two other ancient sites lie on the shores of the second great bay that with Moudros practically chomps the island in half. Hephaistia was once its most important city, but the *Rough Guide* gives it short shrift: "nothing much to interest the nonspecialist." We almost don't take the rough road to it and linger in the delightful village of Kontopouli with its memorable relics of the early 1930s – a faded mansion that housed a Greek-American's grocery, a plaster backdrop for a well, decorated with cherubs, griffons and lions – and a good number of houses painted a startling eggy yellow.

As we draw closer to Hephaistia, a bedraggled bare hillside next to desolate salt flats, we see a smart gravel path leading up to where archaeologists are at work. Limnos is the domain of the Italian School, chosen perhaps because the island's burial customs resemble those of the Etruscans. They've been here, apart from interruptions, for almost eighty years, and have unearthed baths, the main shrine, city walls and Roman houses. These are staggeringly boring to the layman, but beyond them lies a prize: a gorgeous theatre, with Hellenistic foundations and Roman additions, whose pale russet seats seem one with the hillside. Greek archaeologists have been restoring it since 2001 and they were preparing for its "unveiling". They were very protective of it but we persuaded them to let us tiptoe round so long as we did not scuff the immaculate grey path. This gem should not be missed.

At Kabiria, facing Hephaistia on the other side of the bay, there is nothing left of what was once the largest sanctuary to the (pre-Greek) Great Gods, but the location is still majestic. The road to it passes an abandoned hotel/bungalow complex. Built with state subsidies by a well-known industrialist, it was constructed so cheaply, serious cracks appeared during its first and only year of operation. Consider it a monument to the goddess Scandal.

Kabiria's ceremonial hall is but an enormous floor with a few truncated columns on the edge of a dramatic rocky coast. If you are sure of foot, walk down to the rocks above Philoktetes' cave. They conceal a very uncomfortable hole where the legendary Trojan War archer allegedly spent ten years, recovering from a gangrenous snake bite. Myths apart, the swimming here is fantastic.

During these explorations we discovered that the best place to have lunch was at Kotsinas, where there are two waterfront tavernas cooled by a breeze almost as delicious as their steamed mussels. The waiters will tell you to visit the spring concealed inside the nearby mound which is labelled Kastro. The castle exists in name only; the spring is but a well 60 steps under the ground. The bronze statue of teenaged Maroula brandishing her father's sword crowns the mound. When the Turks killed him, she led the fight to defend the castle in 1478. Needless to say, they eventually took it anyway.

Romeikos Yialos, viewed from the Castle, is lined with shaded tavernas

Though we spent our days trying to take in all of Limnos – the sand dunes in the north at Gomati, the startling pink rivulets of oleanders in the bleached hills, pretty beaches at Nevgati and Thanos – we were always happiest at Myrina. For one thing, it has not one but two water-

fronts that start on either side of castle rock. Romeikos Yialos (Greek Beach) is invisible from the port. Here stately 19th century homes look onto a long stretch of wheat-hued shingle paralleled by a string of tavernas. Midway down is the museum, stocked with finds that illuminate

Recyled building blocks in a hut near Hephaistia

those mysterious ancient sites. On the other side, Tourkikos Yialos (Turkish Beach) extends beyond the port with finer sand but humbler houses. Myrina is best viewed from the castle, from where you can sometimes see Mount Athos. As an added bonus, roe deer graze silently amidst the lichen-splattered rocks.

But strolling the streets brings you into contact with Limnos' main asset – its people. Invariably chatty and cheerful, they talked to us about snowy winters, sea-washed cheese, the differences between four kinds of almond-based sweets, where to find Limnos wine in Athens…

As we waited for the boat to Samothrace, the clock chimed 9 at ten past the hour. Just my kind of place; we would return. ○

How to get there

Getting there is definitely not half the fun. Olympic schedules a woefully inadequate two flights a day from Athens – at 5:50 am and 9:15 pm – on small planes seating 40-something passengers. Limnos is considered unprofitable, so Aegean doesn't even serve it. As for ships, there are 3-4 sailings per week from Lavrio or Piraeus and the crossing takes from 12 to 24 (!) hours, depending on the number of intervening stops. Information regarding schedules seems to be guarded under the official secrets act, so summer sailings proved impossible to determine until late June. There are probably three boats a week to Lesvos and Samothrace. Useful numbers: Saos Lines Lavrio (22920 26040), Limnos Port Authority (22540 22225), Petrides Tours (22540 22039/ 22998)

Where to stay (area code 22540)

We stayed at the reasonably priced *Nefeli Apartments*, under the entrance to the castle. Renovated in 2005, it has six comfortable apartments. There are wonderful views from the terrace and downtown is a short (5-10 minutes) walk away. (23551, 22825). On the very upscale end of Limnos accommodation is *Porto Myrina Palace*, elegant and understated with bungalows, beach, pool and sports, grouped around the low walls of the ancient sanctuary of Artemis, around the point from Romeikos Yialos (24805).

Where to eat

Everything we ate in Limnos was superlative, from the steamed mussels on the half shell to a perfectly grilled *sinagrida*, delectable octopus and sardines in vine leaves. Baby *vlita* (summer greens), fried local cheese, salads were all exceptional and the light, fragrant Limnos *moschato* wine, served from the barrel throughout the island, must be the best "loose" wine in Greece. In Myrina, we dined beautifully at two places on the port-side waterfront but failed to notice their names. *Kosmos* at Romeikos Yialos had excellent service and a tank full of lobsters, while *To Koralli* at Kotsinas produced two superb fishful lunches for a quarter of what they would cost in Athens.

Samothraki:
a goat song to the moon

Samothraki is almost all
mountain (the pre-Greek
"samos" means "high")
and walking on the Moon
is another matter,
as we would find out.

"We don't have much traffic here, but watch out for the wild goats. They cause an accident or two every summer," said the rentacar agent when we arrived on Samothraki (Samothrace). "And don't park your car under a tree. The goats will climb on the roof to get at the leaves."

We haven't come here to worry about goats. We've loftier things in mind – a walk on the Moon, a visit to the sanctuary of the Great Gods. This little island has been niggling at my imagination ever since I first saw the Winged Victory in the Louvre, about to take off above a ring of admirers. And when in March I told my niece, M, that the island's mountain range is

Samothraki's rivers more than compensate
for its lack of good beaches

called Fengari, she announced she was coming too. "I will bring A (her science writer husband). Remember when he booked a room in the first hotel to open on the Moon? This will probably be as close as he'll ever get to it."

We spent the two-hour boat ride from Limnos on deck, eyes peeled for the first glimpse of Moon Mountain, where Poseidon sat to watch the Trojan War. Mists enveloped it on that hazy morning and all we glimpsed were low golden-stubbled hills, a sahara of wheat dunes remarkably similar to the landscape we had just left. Kamariotissa, Samothraki's port and only anchorage, lived up to the descriptions in the guidebooks, which unanimously urge readers to leave this "not the most captivating of towns" as soon as possible.

But we can't leave. There's been a mixup about the car, which we were told to pick up "at the café with the curtains". Curious directions but its white draperies big as spinnakers were unmistakable on the low key waterfront. Another boat has arrived in the meantime and drowsy Kamariotissa is as frantic as Bloomingdale's on Christmas eve. By the look and sound of it every passenger is clamouring for wheels. And our agent has left a flunky in charge who pretends he knows nothing. It is not the most auspicious of introductions. We wait. The men console themselves with ouzos and M and I set

off on a fruitless quest for up-to-date ferry/hydrofoil schedules. When the agent appears after an hour or so, he offers us not one but two cars. He also says the summer Flying Dolphin timetable has just been released in Alexandroupoli and Samothraki will have it by tomorrow. This is the 9th of July!

He points us in the direction of the island's only petrol station and X's the map where our hotel is. Almost perfectly round and very small, Samothraki is split down the middle into the yin south – typically Aegean sunburnt with olives and fields – and the yang north – wet, wild and crammed with trees. The roads are mostly excellent but there are not very many of them. One skirts three-quarters of the coast, two venture inland to Hora and a few others connect the island's twelve tiny villages. It's impossible to get lost in a car. But Samothraki is almost all mountain (the pre-Greek "samos" means "high") and walking on the Moon is another matter, as we would find out.

All the guidebooks agree that Therma/Loutra, on the middle of the north coast, is the best place to stay and they are right. This is a spa with a difference. Although its hot sulphurous baths are recommended for aching old limbs, international hippies in hiking boots outnumber arthritic Greeks in flipflops. Posters for the July and August New Age youth festivals

Hora, built in the shadow of the Moon

hang in every shop. Lively cafés and tavernas stay open well past midnight.

This is also where the jungle begins, a riot of greenery that cannot be matched by any Greek island. In addition to the steamy springs, some 20 rivers tumble through this corner of it. Even Pelion seems barren in comparison. Fruit trees, plane trees, chestnuts and walnuts crowd to-gether to create dense shade. Hydrangeas with their big pink heads are as ubiquitous as gerani-ums elsewhere in Greece. Roses, oleanders, flowering vines all but bury our hotel outside the village. We breathe a contented sigh as Samothraki starts to weave its magic.

In the afternoon, we go for a swim at Ther-ma's black stone beach. An eccentric newspaper

Pachia Ammos – "fat sands" – is a very relative term

editor in a recent series on favourite beaches wrote that he preferred Therma because it was so uncomfortable, the sea so cold he was likely to be alone. Perhaps that was wishful thinking, for today a few dozen people are splashing happily and the water temperature is more than acceptable. Still, it is true that no one travels to Samothraki just to swim. Most of the inhospitable shoreline is little better than a skinny ribbon of black and white pebbles of varying sharpness. Its only two accessible sandy strands lie at the beginning and end of the coast road. At Kipos, there is no hint of the garden implied in its name, and at Pachia Ammos, "fat sands" is a very relative term, but they satisfy any yearnings for traditional Greek summer scenery nonetheless.

It has been said that Samothraki's mountain is so awesome and dramatic that everything manmade palls in comparison. Everything except the Sanctuary of the Great Gods. The island may have no indigenous architectural masterpieces. Magnificent churches and mansions are scarce; the island was too poor, conditions too harsh to permit those luxuries. But the Sanctuary has all you want in an ancient site: romantic setting, sense of place, sufficient remains to kindle your interest, freedom to wander and an enigmatic past.

The worship of the Great Gods was a mystery religion, its origins pre-Greek. The earliest names of the gods themselves, collectively known as Kabeiroi, sound strange and unfamiliar to our ears, and like that of the God of Abraham were not spoken. In fact, the word may derive from the Semitic *kabir*, pl. *kabirim*, which means "Almighty". There were four of them, with the Great Mother, Axieros, predominant. She came to be associated with Cybele or Demeter. The others were her spouse, the fertility god Kadmilos identified with Hermes, and Axiokersos and Axiokersa, who later merged with Hades and Persephone. Anatolian deities, they were virtually unknown on the mainland.

As at Eleusis, near Athens, secret rituals took place here annually but the initiates' lips were sealed and scholars can only make educated guesses as to the proceedings. What they do know is that they were ecumenical; anyone could take part, regardless of sex, social status, nationality or age. There were two levels of initiation and they seem to have had some moral criteria, which incorporated confession and absolution, but were not all solemn. The torchlight ceremonies concluded with copious eating and drinking. Throughout the Greek and Roman era, the mysteries were made more mysterious by being conducted in the mumbo-jumbo of the original pre-Greek language, much as Latin was in the Roman Catholic church until recently.

A visit to the site begins with a small museum whose showpiece is a plaster cast of the famous Victory. Carved from Parian marble by the Rhodian sculptor Pythokritos in the 2nd century BC, she decorated a fountain above the main temple. In 1863 a Frenchman named Champoiseau abducted her, returning a few years later to collect the marble ship-prow on which she had balanced.

Although the Sanctuary is far older, the ruins are mainly Hellenistic and Roman. Chunks of marble lie along the path, which leads slowly to the focal point – the five white columns of the temple proper – and then up and around so you see them from many different angles. Surrounded by trees, interrupted by pink oleanders, they demand to be photographed from

Although the sanctuary is far older, the ruins are mainly Hellenistic and Roman

each perspective. But there are many other unusual ruins – the biggest circular building in ancient Greece dedicated by Queen Arsinoe of Egypt, a palace, an enormous colonnade, the very damaged fountain where Victory presided, a small theatre – in an intriguing array of masonry and colours. Above them all reign the formidable peaks of the Moon, still capable of

inducing a shiver in the hot July sun.

Afterwards, on the way to Kipos beach, a sign for Karydies taverna beckoned us into the hills. Goats watched our progress, one from the fork of a plane tree, as we crawled past well nibbled bushes, back into forest and finally to tamed garden. We sat ourselves next to a hedge of hydrangeas and listened to Yorgo re-

The real thing
is in the Louvre

Meanwhile, I kept exploring near our hotel. While the others napped, I was discovering waterfalls, rock pools and rivers. At the sign for Gria Vathra/Christos, one step off the sunlit road lands you in a dark forest peopled by humongous plane trees. Contorted, bulbous trunks, roots as tangled as the mops of a hundred Medusas on a bad hair day, branches that could easily reach out and grab you – I felt like a very tiny Hobbit but pressed on. After following a few wrong arrows, I found the appropriately named Old Lady's Basin and let its deliciously icy small cataract shower away the spookiness.

I never did find Christos, a ruined monastery near another river. Samothraki has extraordinary beauty spots but seems unwilling to share them. Few destinations are named, arrows peter out.

Only one path is very clearly marked. It follows the course of the Fonias river up to a series of deep pools and a lovely waterfall. A young man at its start was collecting an optional euro for keeping the place clean and dispensing the warnings you hear whenever you read or talk about walks in Samothraki: "The path con-

cite the islanders' manifold methods of keeping the goat population under control: goat baked in wax paper, stuffed goat, fried, grilled, boiled with (divine) pilaff, roast, stewed with tomatoes or with lemon, liver and head. Delicious they were, too, but Karydies' home-grown vegetables, omelettes and home-baked bread were also worth the detour. We'd stumbled upon the best restaurant on the island.

Reviving in Old Lady's Basin

path to the first falls. Threaded by elaborate roots, shaded by outrageous branches, this transit ought to be labelled "plane-tree museum". It is even more exciting than the goal, especially if people are sprawled like basking walruses on the flat rocks. We slipped past them into the clear pool to view the mini-Niagara that fills it.

We never did get to walk on the Moon. All the approaches to the 1600 m peak are rated "difficult", requiring a guide unless you are an experienced goat and taking from eight to nine hours, round trip. The closest we managed was a stroll through Hora, straight up from the port. Built in the mountain's shadow, this is no carefree island capital even in summer. Though flowers cascade from window sills and doorsteps, many of the small granite houses are deserted, shops practically nonexistent. Photos on the walls of the small museum show the struggle to survive inside the walls of the now crumbled Genoese fortress. Many locals are as stony as their surroundings, no doubt toughened by their isolation.

The Moon must be an exacting place to live but it's a fascinating place to visit. Even if you only snoop around its lower regions. ○

tinues after the first waterfall, but we advise you not to take it; it's not well marked and it's dangerous."

"Why is it called Killer river?" I asked, expecting a romantic tale of misplaced love and betrayal .

"Because this river when it's flooded sweeps up everything in its path – goats, people, cars. A few years ago a car it swept out to sea ended up on a beach in Thasos."

It takes about 45 minutes to walk up the

How to get there

Stuck way off in the northeast Aegean, Samothraki is reached most easily by hydrofoil from Alexandroupoli, which does have an airport. In summer these can run more than once a day, but extracting their schedule and that of the erratic ferries to and from Alexandroupoli, Limnos or Kavala can be diabolically difficult, even when you are on the island.

Where to stay (area code 25510)

Hotels are not Samothraki's strong point. The local Ritz is the newish *Kastro Hotel* on the coast at Palaiopoli near the Sanctuary. Its simple rooms are improved by balconies overlooking the pool or sea (89400). We stayed at pretty *Mariva Bungalows* (98230), which we dubbed Fawlty Towers because of its "killer" beds with sharp stone edges and casual attitude towards upkeep. There are plenty of rooms in and around Therma. The young stay at the two Multilary (ie Municipal) campsites not far from Therma in another plane tree forest, where the festivals are held.

Where to eat

Samothraki is a carnivore's dream, justifying the existence of all those goats. Apart from our favourite place, *Karydies* (98266) at Mesa Meria, there are several other agreeable tavernas: *I Gefyra*, *Oi Katarraktes* and *To Perivoli tou Ouranou* between Therma and Gria Vathra; at Pachia Ammos; and in Hora, either *1900* or *Kastro* in the main square and *Pyrgos* next to the castle for drinks and snacks.

B I B L I O G R A P H Y

Manolis Andronikos, *Vergina, The Royal Tombs* (Ekdotike Athenon, Athens, 1984).

Robin Barber, *Blue Guide Greece* (A. & C. Black, London, 1995).

Pavlos Christostomou & Frangiska Kefallonitou, *Nikopolis* (Ministry of Culture, Archaeological Receipts Fund, Athens, 2001).

Stella Dragou & Christina Saatsoglou-Paliadeli, *Vergina, Wandering through the Ancient Site* (Ministry of Culture, Archaeological Receipts Fund, Athens, 2004).

Epirus (Explorer S.A., Athens, 2002) (in Greek).

Eleni Gage, *North of Ithaka* (Bantam Books, London, 2005).

Nicholas Gage, *Eleni* (Random House, New York, 1983).

Nicholas Gage, *Hellas*, A Portrait of Greece (Efstathiadis Group, Athens, 1987).

Greece, Only the Best (Axon Ekdotiki, Maroussi, 2001) (in Greek).

Greek Islands (Lonely Planet, London, 2004).

Herodotus, *The Histories*, trans. Robin Waterfield (Oxford, Oxford University Press, 1998).

Antonis Iordanoglou, *Unexplored Central Macedonia* (Road Editions, Athens, 2002) (in Greek).

Antonis Iordanoglou, *Unexplored Western Macedonia* (Road Editions, Athens, 2002) (in Greek).

Dimitris Konstantios, *The Kastro of Ioannina* (Ministry of Culture, Archaeological Receipts Fund, Athens, 1997).

Giannis Kyritsis, *O Olympos tou Boissonas* (Muncipality of Litohoro, Zarzoni Editions, Thessaloniki, no date).

Osbert Lancaster, *Classical Landscape with Figures* (John Murray, London, 1975).

Dimitrios Lazaridis, *Amphipolis* (Ministry of Culture, Archaeological Receipts Fund, Athens, 1997).

Patrick Leigh Fermor, *Roumeli* (Penguin, London, 1987).

Lemnos, The Island of Hephaestus (Toubis, Athens, 2005).

Diana Farr Louis, *Corfu, Only the Best* (Axon Ekdotiki, Maroussi, 2001).

Diana Farr Louis & June Marinos, *Prospero's Kitchen, Mediterranean Cooking of the Ionian Islands from Corfu to Kythera* (M. Evans & Co., New York, 1995).

Nikos Manessis, *The Illustrated Greek Wine Book* (Olive Press Publications, Corfu, 2000).

D. Matsas & A. Bakirtzis, *Samothrace, A Short Cultural Guide* (Municipality of Samothrace, Athens, 2001).

Mark Mazower, *Salonica, City of Ghosts* (Harper Collins, London, 2004).

Eric Newby, *On the Shores of the Mediterranean* (Picador, London, 1984).

Hilary Whitton Paipeti, *The Second Book of Corfu Walks* (Hermes Press and Production, Corfu, 1999).

Hilary Whitton Paipeti, *In the Footsteps of Lawrence Durrell and Gerald Durrell in Corfu (1935-39), A Modern Guidebook* (Hermes Press and Production, Corfu, 1998).

Dimitrios Pandermalis, *Dion* (Adam Editions, Athens, 1997).

Barbara N. Papadopoulou, *The Monasteries of the Island of Ioannina* (Holy Monastery of Eleousa, Ioannina, 2004).

Penguin Guide to Greece 1990 (New York, 1990).

Plutarch, *The Age of Alexander* (Penguin Classics, London, 1973).

Stephanos Psimenos, *Unexplored Thessaly* (Road Editions, Athens, 2003) (in Greek)

David Ramshaw, *Halkidiki, walking-wandern* (Halkidiki Hotel Association, Thessaloniki, 2000).

Noel Rochford, *Landscapes of Corfu* (Sunflower Books, London, 1999).

Routard Grèce Continentale (Hachette, Paris, 2004).

Tim Salmon, *The Unwritten Places* (Lycabettus Press, Athens, 1993).

"Samothraki, An Ecotourist and Trekking Map" (Oikotopia, Dimotiki Epiheirisi Anaptyxis Samothrakis).

Smouldering Limnos, ed. Evangelia Kypraiou (Ministry of Culture, Archaeological Receipts Fund, Athens, 2000).

Ta Loutra tis Elladas (Kastaniotis, Athens, 2001).

Thraki/Samothraki, Only the Best (Axon Ekdotiki, Maroussi, 2001) (in Greek).

Thessaloniki, Only the Best (Axon Ekdotiki, Maroussi, 2000) (In Greek).

Santo Tine & Antonella Traverso, *Poliochni, The Earliest Town in Europe* (Archaeological Society at Athens, Athens, 2001).

Michael Ward, *Greek Assignments, SOE 1943-1948 UNSCOB* (Lycabettus Press, Athens, 1992).

Alexandros Zaousis, *I Tragiki Anametrisi*, vol. 1 (Okeanida, Athens, 1992).

PHOTO CREDITS

The photographs in this book are by:
Argyris Carras on the cover and on pages
6-7, 34-35, 38, 122, 237;
Michael Cullen on pages 4-5, 12, 18, 20, 21,
46, 52-53, 54-55, 56-57, 58, 60, 74, 114,
116-117, 118-119, 136, 137, 140, 141, 142,
144, 146 and 157;
Diana Farr Louis on pages 19, 23, 28, 29,
37, 39, 40-41, 44, 51, 62, 67, 70, 71, 72, 77,
78, 79, 80-81, 85, 87, 88, 92-93, 97, 100,
101, 103, 105, 110-111, 112-113, 115, 120,
121, 125, 126-127, 128, 129, 130, 133, 134,
138-139, 149, 151, 152, 153, 154, 159(l),
161(d), 171, 173, 175, 176, 177, 186, 187,
188, 191, 193, 196, 198, 203, 204-205, 206,
212, 217, 219, 220, 222, 225, 227, 230, 231,
232, 235, 236, 238-239, 240, 242, 243, 244,
245, 248, 253, 254-255, 256, 257, 259, 260,
262, 263, 264-265, 267, 269, 271, 272, 277,
278, 281, 282, 283.
All other images come from Motionteam,
EPA, AP, Icon, Eurokinissi, Avaton, Reuters.

Editor: Thrasy Petropoulos
Design: Poppy Alexiou & Alexandra Drossou
Pre-press and printing: Multimedia S.A.

Series Editor: John Psaropoulos